Ready® | 2

Mathematics
PRACTICE AND
PROBLEM SOLVING

Editorial Director: Cynthia Tripp
Cover Designer and Illustrator: Matt Pollock
Illustrator: Sam Valentino
Photography Credit: wk1003mike/Shutterstock (front cover background)

NOT FOR RESALE

ISBN 978-0-7609-9223-4
©2015—Curriculum Associates, LLC
North Billerica, MA 01862

Table of Contents

Family Letter available with every lesson.

Family Letter available with every lesson.

Family Letter available with every lesson.

Dear Family,

This week your child is exploring using fact families to solve addition and subtraction problems with mental math.

A **fact family** is a group of related number sentences that use the same numbers, but in a different order.

$$9 + 6 = 15 \qquad 15 - 9 = 6$$
$$6 + 9 = 15 \qquad 15 - 6 = 9$$

When asked to find $15 - 9$ using mental math, your child can solve a related fact that he or she may find easier. $15 - 9 = ?$ is the same as $9 + ? = 15$, and if your child knows that $9 + 6 = 15$, then he or she knows $15 - 9 = 6$.

Another strategy your child can use is **counting on**. What is $15 - 9$? Using the fact family, you can think of it as $9 + ? = 15$. Count on from 9 to 15.

1	2	3	4	5	6	7	8	⑨	10 /
11 /	12 /	13 /	14 /	15 /	16	17	18	19	20

You counted on 6 numbers.
$9 + 6 = 15$, so $15 - 9 = 6$.

Invite your child to share what he or she knows about using fact families by doing the following activity together.

NEXT

Lesson 1 Understand Mental Math Strategies (Fact Families)   **1**

Fact Family Activity

Work with your child to create fact family cards, by cutting out the facts below and coloring the backs, or by writing the facts on index cards.

- Each player chooses one of the single-number cards (14 or 17) and places it face-up in front of him or her. Shuffle the fact cards. Place them face-down in 2 rows with 4 cards in each row.

- Players take turns flipping over two cards.
  - If either of the cards are not in the same fact family as the player's number card, then put them both back face down.
  - If both of the cards are in the same fact family as the number card, then the player keeps the cards.

- The first player to find the 4 cards that make a family that goes with his or her number card wins.

$8 + 6 = 14$	$6 + 8 = 14$	$14 - 8 = 6$
$14 - 6 = 8$	$9 + 8 = 17$	$8 + 9 = 17$
$17 - 9 = 8$	$17 - 8 = 9$	14 17

Understand
Mental Math Strategies (Fact Families)

Name: _____

Prerequisite: **How can adding help you subtract?**

Study the example showing how adding helps you subtract. Then solve Problems 1–7.

Example

Solve 9 − 5.

Make a number bond.

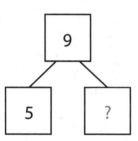

Write an addition problem. Solve.

5 + **?** = 9

5 + **4** = 9

Then solve the subtraction.

9 − 5 = **4**

---

1 Circle the number bond for 13 − 6.

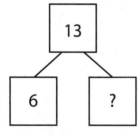 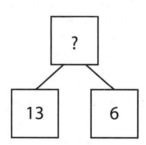

2 Complete the number bond. Write four number sentences.

_____ + _____ = 13   13 − _____ = _____

13 = _____ + _____   _____ = 13 − _____

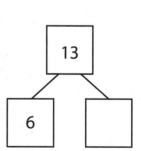

Solve.

3 Complete the number bond to show
$15 - 6 = \boxed{?}$.

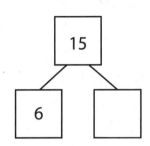

4 Write an addition sentence for the number bond in Problem 3. Then complete the subtraction sentence.

_____ + _____ = _____

$15 - 6 =$ _____

5 Complete the number bond to show
$16 - 7 = \boxed{?}$.

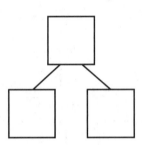

6 Write the fact family for the number bond in Problem 5.

_____ + _____ = _____ 　　　 _____ + _____ = _____

_____ − _____ = _____ 　　　 _____ − _____ = _____

7 Show how to find $14 - 8 = \boxed{?}$ using addition.

Show your work.

Vocabulary

fact family
a group of facts that all use the same three numbers.

Name: _____

Use Different Strategies to Subtract

Study how the example shows counting on to subtract in your head. Then solve Problems 1–6.

> **Example**
>
> $13 - 9 = ?$
>
> Think of it as $9 + \boxed{?} = 13$.
>
> Count on to get from 9 to 13.
>
> | ⑨ | 10 | 11 | 12 | 13 |
> |---|----|----|----|----|
> | | / | / | / | / |
>
> The marks show how many you counted on.
>
> Solve the addition problem. $9 + 4 = 13$
>
> Solve the subtraction problem. $13 - 9 = 4$

1 Fill in the blanks in each number sentence.

$9 - 4 = \boxed{?}$ is the same as _____ $+ \boxed{?} =$ _____.

$11 - 7 = \boxed{?}$ is the same as _____ $+ \boxed{?} =$ _____.

$8 - 3 = \boxed{?}$ is the same as _____ $+ \boxed{?} =$ _____.

$15 - 8 = \boxed{?}$ is the same as _____ $+ \boxed{?} =$ _____.

2 Choose one subtraction number sentence from Problem 1. Do you think it is faster to solve it using addition facts or counting on? Explain.

_____

_____

_____

Solve.

3 Fill in the blanks in the number sentence.

12 − 7 = $\boxed{?}$ is the same as _____ + $\boxed{?}$ = _____ .

4 Fill in the number bond to find
12 − 7 = $\boxed{?}$. Then write your answer.

12 − 7 = _____

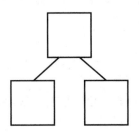

5 Show a different way to find 12 − 7.

Show your work.

12 − 7 = _____

6 In Problems 4 and 5 you used two different strategies to find 12 − 7 = $\boxed{?}$. Which strategy do you think is faster to do in your head? Explain.

_____

_____

_____

_____

6   **Lesson 1** Understand Mental Math Strategies (Fact Families)

Name: _____

Reason and Write

Look at the example. Underline a part that you think makes it a good answer.

Example

Choose a problem.

$9 - 6 = ?$ $12 - 4 = ?$

$14 - 5 = ?$ $15 - 8 = ?$

1. Show how to solve the problem by drawing a picture of an open number line.

2. Explain how to use the number line to solve the problem.

Show.

$12 - 4 = ?$

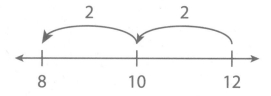

Explain.

I pictured an open number line. I started with 12.

First I subtracted 2 to make 10. Then I subtracted

2 more to subtract a total of 4. Since I ended up

on 8, I know that $12 - 4 = 8$.

Where does the example . . .

- show the selected problem?

- show the strategy?

- explain the strategy?

Lesson 1 Understand Mental Math Strategies (Fact Families)

Solve the problem. Use what you learned from the example.

Choose a problem.

$9 - 6 = ?$ $11 - 3 = ?$

$14 - 5 = ?$ $15 - 8 = ?$

1. Show how to solve the problem by drawing a picture of an open number line.

2. Explain how to use the number line to solve the problem.

Show.

Explain.

_____

_____

_____

_____

Did you . . .

• show the selected problem?

• show the strategy?

• explain the strategy?

Dear Family,

This week your child is learning different ways to solve one-step word problems using addition or subtraction.

Consider the following word problem: Alex has 13 carrot sticks. He eats 5 carrot sticks. How many carrot sticks does he have left?

You can model this problem many different ways.

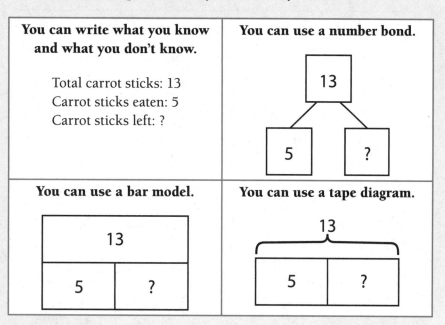

You can write what you know and what you don't know.	**You can use a number bond.**
Total carrot sticks: 13 Carrot sticks eaten: 5 Carrot sticks left: ?	13 5 ?
You can use a bar model.	**You can use a tape diagram.**
13 5 ?	13 5 ?

Each of these models will help you write all the facts of the fact family.

$13 - 5 = ?$	$13 - ? = 5$	$5 + ? = 13$	$? + 5 = 13$

You can solve to find that Alex has 8 carrot sticks left.

Invite your child to share what he or she knows about solving one-step word problems by doing the following activity together.

Solving One-Step Word Problems Activity

Materials: 20 small objects (pennies, buttons, bite-sized crackers);
2 cups or other containers

Take turns making up and solving word problems about the objects.
Each time, say a number sentence to describe the problem. Ask your
child to name all the related number sentences in the same fact family.
Encourage your child to check his or her work by counting.

Example: Put 11 pennies in one cup and 6 on the table. Then ask your
child to solve these four problems.

- How many coins are there in all? (11 + 6 = 17)

11 + 6 = 17	6 + 11 = 17	17 − 11 = 6	17 − 6 = 11

- How many more pennies are in the cup than on the table?
  (11 − 6 = 5)

11 − 6 = 5	11 − 5 = 6	5 + 6 = 11	6 + 5 = 11

- If I take away 2 pennies from the cup, how many pennies will be
  left in the cup? (11 − 2 = 9)

11 − 2 = 9	11 − 9 = 2	2 + 9 = 11	9 + 2 = 11

- How many pennies will I need to put on the table to have
  10 pennies on the table? (10 − 6 = 4)

10 − 6 = 4	10 − 4 = 6	4 + 6 = 10	6 + 4 = 10

Solve One-Step Word Problems

Name: _____

Study the example showing how to use a bar model to solve a word problem. Then solve Problems 1–6.

Example

Ed has 4 black crayons and 9 green crayons. How many more green crayons are there?

Draw a picture to show what you know.

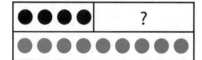

Use the picture to write a number sentence. Solve.

$4 + ? = 9$

$4 + 5 = 9$

There are 5 more green crayons.

1 Use a number bond to model the Example problem. Write each number or symbol in the correct box.

 ? 4 9

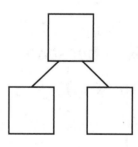

2 Write a complete fact family for the Example problem.

_____

Solve.

3 Troy has 8 points in a game. Then he gets more points. Now he has 12 points. How many more points does he get?

8 + _____ = 12

Troy gets _____ more points.

| 7 | 8 | 9 | 10 | 11 | 12 | 13 | 14 |

4 Look at Problem 3. Model it using a number bond. Then write a subtraction sentence.

_____ − _____ = _____

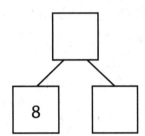

5 Liz has 15 CDs. 9 are music CDs. The rest are story CDs. How many are story CDs?
Show your work.

Number sentence: _____

There are _____ story CDs.

6 There are 13 cartons of milk and 6 straws. How many fewer straws are there?
Show your work.

Number sentence: _____

There are _____ fewer straws.

Name: _____

Solve Take-Apart Word Problems

Study the example showing one way to solve a take-apart word problem. Then solve Problems 1–5.

Example

A cart has 14 books. There are 6 on the bottom shelf. The rest are on the top shelf. How many books are on the top shelf?

You can use a tape diagram.

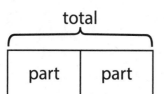

Write what you know.

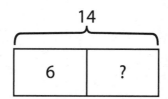

Write a number sentence. Solve.

$14 - 6 = ?$

$14 - 6 = 8$

There are 8 books on the top shelf.

---

1 Complete the tape diagram for the Example problem. Then complete the number sentence.

$14 = \underline{\hspace{1cm}} + \underline{\hspace{1cm}}$

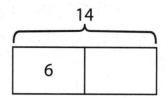

2 Look at the number sentence you wrote in Problem 1. Explain what your number sentence says about the books in the Example.

_____

_____

_____

Solve.

3 Rik picked 16 apples. He keeps 9 apples. He gives the rest to friends. How many apples does Rik give his friends?

Circle *Yes* or *No* to show if the information is given in the problem.

a. the number of
apples Rik picked   Yes   No

b. the number of apples
Rik gives his friends   Yes   No

c. the number of
apples Rik ate   Yes   No

d. the number of
apples Rik keeps   Yes   No

4 Look at Problem 3. Complete a tape diagram and solve the problem. Tell how you found your answer.

Rik gave his friends _____ apples.

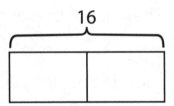

_____

_____

5 There are 11 frogs at the pond. There are 5 frogs in the water. The rest are in the mud. How many frogs are in the mud?

Show your work.

Answer: _____

Name: _____

Solve Comparison Word Problems

Study the example showing a way to solve a comparison word problem. Then solve Problems 1–4.

Example

Maya has 4 hamsters and some mice. She has 3 fewer hamsters than mice. How many mice does Maya have?

Think about what you know.

> There are **3 fewer hamsters** than mice. That means there are **3 more mice** than hamsters.

Draw a picture.

hamsters

mice

Write a number sentence. $4 + 3 = 7$

Maya has 7 mice.

1 There are 4 fewer markers than crayons. Circle *fewer* or *more* to complete each sentence.

There are 4 **fewer/more** markers than crayons.

That means there are 4 **fewer/more** crayons than markers.

Solve.

2 There are 4 fewer markers than crayons. There are 6 markers. How many crayons are there?

Show your work.

Answer: _____

3 There are 8 children standing. There are 3 fewer children standing than sitting. How many children are sitting? Circle the correct answer.

A 3   **C** 8

B 5   **D** 11

4 Dara has 12 red counters. She has 7 more red counters than yellow counters. How many yellow counters does Dara have?

Show your work.

Answer: _____

Name: _____

Solve Different Kinds of Word Problems

Solve the problems.

1 Sid has 17 flowers. There are 8 blue flowers. The rest are yellow. How many flowers are yellow?

Circle *Yes* or *No* to show if the information is given in the problem.

It could be helpful to underline the information given in the problem.

a. the number of yellow flowers   Yes   No

b. the number of red flowers   Yes   No

c. the number of blue flowers   Yes   No

d. the total number of flowers   Yes   No

2 Sid has 17 flowers. There are 8 blue flowers. The rest are yellow. How many flowers are yellow?

Circle the correct answer.

You can add or subtract to find the answer.

A 8   **C** 17

B 9   **D** 20

Solve.

3 There are 9 dancers in a play. There are 3 more dancers than singers in the play. How many singers are in the play?

Show your work.

Are there more dancers or singers in the play?

Answer: _____

4 Lin has 4 pinecones and some acorns. She has 7 fewer pinecones than acorns. How many acorns does Lin have? Circle the correct answer.

Does Lin have more pinecones or acorns?

A 3   **C** 7

B 4   **D** 11

Tom chose **A**. This is wrong. How did Tom get his answer?

_____

_____

_____

_____

Dear Family,

This week your child is exploring how using the "make a 10" strategy helps when adding or subtracting with mental math.

Adding and subtracting can be easier when one number is 10. By breaking apart a number, you can add or subtract to make 10 and then add or subtract the rest.

Add 6 + 8.

Think of 8 as 4 + 4.

Add 6 and 4 to make 10.

Add the other 4.

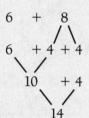

Adding 10 + 4 is an easier problem to solve mentally:
10 + 4 = 14, so
6 + 8 = 14.

The "make a 10" strategy can be modeled with an **open number line** (a number line not drawn to scale, with only the numbers important to the problem labeled).

15 − 8 = ? (Think of 8 as 5 + 3.)
15 − 5 = 10
10 − 3 = 7

Subtract 5 to get to 10.
Then subtract the remaining 3.

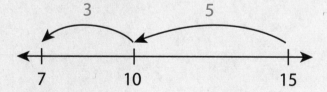

15 − 8 = 7

Invite your child to share what he or she knows about making a 10 by doing the following activity together.

Lesson 3 Understand Mental Math Strategies (Make a Ten)   **19**

Making a Ten Activity

Play the following game with your child to practice adding using mental math.

- Begin by holding up 6 fingers. Ask your child to add 9 to that number.

- Have your child add the numbers by "making a 10" and using your fingers to model the process. (For example, your child might start by adding 4 and putting the rest of your fingers up, and then adding 5 of his or her own fingers, to model adding 9.)

- Ask your child to check the answer by counting the fingers.

- Repeat with other numbers of fingers, playing for about 5 minutes.

If I hold up 8 fingers, how can I add 7 by making a 10?

Name: _____

Prerequisite: How does thinking about number paths help you add and subtract in your head?

Study the example showing the make a ten strategy on a number path. Then solve Problems 1–6.

Example

Add 8 + 5.

Think of a number path.
Start at 8.
Add 2 to make 10.

You need to add 3 more.

5 = **2** + **3**

So, 8 + 5 = 13.

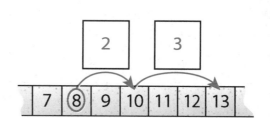

1 Make a ten to add 9 + 6. First write all the number partners of 6.

_____

2 Make a ten. Fill in the missing numbers.

  9 + 6 = ?

  9 + _____ = 10 and 10 + _____ = _____

So, 9 + 6 = _____ .

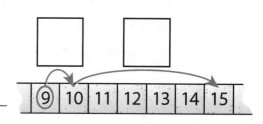

Solve.

3 Subtract. Fill in the missing numbers.

$11 - 4 = ?$

$4 = 3 + 1$

So, $11 - 4 =$ _____.

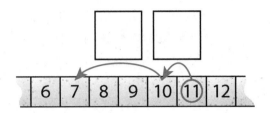

4 Use 2 and 2 for the number partners instead in Problem 3. What is different?

_____

_____

_____

_____

5 Subtract. Fill in the missing numbers.

$14 - 8 = ?$

$8 =$ _____ $+$ _____

So, $14 - 8 =$ _____.

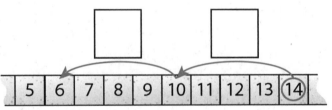

6 How is making a ten to add the same as making a ten to subtract? How is it different?

_____

_____

_____

Explore the Make a Ten Strategy

Study how the example shows making a ten to add. Then solve Problems 1–6.

Example

$8 + 7 = ?$

$8 + \textbf{2} + ?$

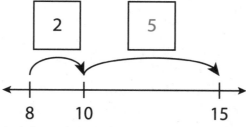

The partners 8 and 2 make 10.

$8 + 7 = ?$

$8 + 2 + \textbf{5}$

Add 5, the other partner of 7.

So, $8 + 7 = 15$.

---

1 Fill in the missing numbers to find $9 + 4$.

$9 + \quad 4 = ?$

$9 + \boxed{} + \boxed{}$

So, $9 + 4 =$ _____.

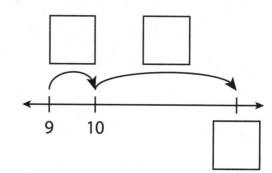

2 Look at the open number line in Problem 1. How would you change the numbers to show $9 + 5$?

_____

Solve.

3 Make a ten to subtract. Fill in the missing numbers to show $12 - 4 = 8$.

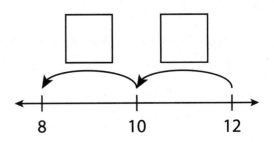

4 Complete the number sentences.

$12 -$ ☐ $= 10$ $16 -$ ☐ $= 10$

$13 -$ ☐ $= 10$ $15 -$ ☐ $= 10$

5 Fill in the missing numbers to find $15 - 9$.

$15 - 9 = ?$

$15 - 9 =$ ☐

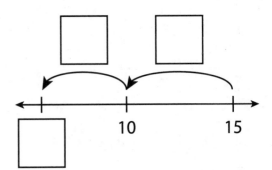

6 Jan circled the problems that she cannot solve in her head by making a ten.

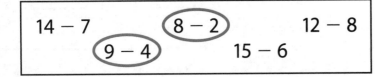

Look at all of the problems. Why doesn't Jan make a ten to solve the circled problems?

_____

_____

_____

Name: _____

Reason and Write

Look at the example. Underline a part that you think makes it a good answer.

Example

1. Write an addition sentence you can solve by making a ten.

2. Describe the steps for making a ten to add. Write three or four steps. You can use words and pictures.

$$\underline{\quad 8 \quad} + \underline{\quad 6 \quad} = \underline{\quad 14 \quad}$$

Step 1 Start at 8. Add a number to 8 to make 10. The number to add is 2. $8 + 2 = 10$.

Step 2 Use 2 as a partner. Find the other partner that makes 6. The partners are 2 and 4.

Step 3 Think of moving 2 places on a number line from 8 to 10. Then move 4 more places from 10 to 14.

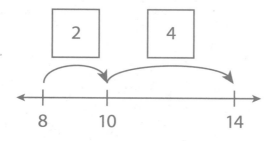

Step 4 The number you end at is your answer. It is 14.

Where does the example . . .

- show the addition sentence?

- use words to explain?

- use numbers to explain?

- use a picture to explain?

Solve the problem. Use what you learned from the example.

1. Write a subtraction sentence you can solve by making a ten.

2. Describe the steps for making a ten to subtract. Write three or four steps. You can use words and pictures.

Show your work.

Did you . . .
- show the addition sentence?
- use words to explain?
- use numbers to explain?
- use a picture to explain?

Dear Family,

This week your child is exploring odd and even numbers.

You can tell whether a number is odd or even by trying to make either groups of 2 or 2 equal groups.

A number is **even** if you can make either groups of 2 or 2 equal groups and have no leftovers.

8 is even.

10 is even.

A number is **odd** if you make either groups of 2 or equal groups and have 1 leftover.

7 is odd.

9 is odd.

Invite your child to share what he or she knows about odd and even numbers by doing the following activity together.

NEXT

Odds or Evens Activity

Materials: 30 small objects (pennies, buttons, dry pieces of cereal); a bag

Play the Odds or Evens game with your child.

- Have your child choose odds or evens, and take the other category for yourself.

- Put 30 pennies in a bag.

- Have your child reach in and take a handful of pennies.

- Work with your child to count the number of pennies.

- Ask your child whether the number is even or odd.

- Have your child check his or her answer by trying to put the pennies into pairs.

- Help your child record everything on the scorecard below. Play 4 more rounds.

Odds or Evens Game

Round	Number of Pennies	Winner	
1		Odd	Even
2		Odd	Even
3		Odd	Even
4		Odd	Even
5		Odd	Even

Lesson 4 Understand Even and Odd Numbers

Name: _____

Prerequisite: **What are doubles facts and doubles + 1 facts?**

Study the example showing doubles and doubles + 1 facts. Then solve Problems 1–5.

Example

This picture shows two equal groups. You can write a doubles fact to show how many in all.

 4 squares

 4 squares

$4 + 4 = 8$

In this picture, one group has 1 more than the other group. You can write a doubles + 1 fact to show how many in all.

 4 squares

 4 + 1 squares

$4 + 4 + 1 = 9$

1   Circle two equal groups. Then complete the doubles fact to show how many in all.

_____ + _____ = _____

Solve.

2 Circle to show two equal groups of stars with 1 leftover. Then complete the doubles + 1 fact to show how many in all.

_____ + _____ + 1 = _____

3 Circle two equal groups of dots. Then write a doubles fact to show how many in all.

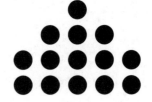

_____ + _____ = _____

4 Look at the two equal groups in Problem 3. How are they alike? How are they different?

_____

_____

_____

_____

5 Complete the doubles + 1 fact. Then tell how you decided what numbers to write.

_____ + _____ + 1 = 13

_____

_____

_____

Name: _____

Identify Even and Odd Numbers

Study how the example shows different ways to decide if a number is odd or even. Then solve Problems 1–6.

Example

The sum of a doubles fact is an even number.

     $3 + 3 = 6$ 6 is an even number.

The sum of a doubles + 1 fact is an odd number.

     $3 + 3 + 1 = 7$ **7** is an odd number.

1 Write a doubles fact for 12. Is 12 odd or even? Circle the correct answer.

odd

_____ + _____ = _____

even

2 Write a doubles + 1 fact for 15. Is 15 odd or even? Circle the correct answer.

odd

_____ + _____ + 1 = _____

even

Vocabulary

even number
an even number of objects can be put into pairs or equal groups.

odd number
an odd number of objects cannot be put into pairs or equal groups without a leftover.

Solve.

3 Circle the even numbers.

    11   14   20   17   16

4 Write a doubles fact for each even number in Problem 3. Fill in the table.

Even Numbers	Doubles Facts

5 Evan has an even number of shells. He has more than 10 shells and less than 15 shells. How many could he have? Tell how you know.

_____

_____

_____

6 Think of the different ways you know to tell if a number is odd or even. Which way do you think you will use most often? Why?

_____

_____

_____

Name: _____

Reason and Write

Look at the example. Underline a part that you think makes it a good answer.

Example

Tell whether 15 is odd or even.

Explain in two different ways why your answer is correct. Use pictures, words, or numbers.

Show your work.

15 is an ____odd____ number.

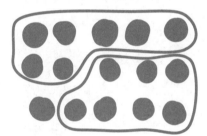

I can't put 15 dots into two equal groups. That means 15 is an odd number.

Also, 15 is one more than 14. I can write a doubles fact for 14. That means I can write a doubles + 1 fact for 15. So, 15 is an odd number.

14 = 7 + 7

15 = 7 + 7 + 1

Where does the example . . .
- show the answer one way?
- show the answer another way?
- use pictures?
- use numbers?

Solve the problem. Use what you learned from the example.

Tell whether 18 is odd or even.

Explain in two different ways why your answer is correct. Use pictures, words, or numbers.

Show your work.

18 is an _____ number.

Did you . . .
- show the answer one way?
- show the answer another way?
- use pictures?
- use numbers?

Dear Family,

This week your child is learning about adding with arrays.

Your child is working with arrays to build skills related to addition.

> **array:** A set of objects arranged in equal rows and equal columns.
> **row:** the horizontal groups of objects in an array.
> **column:** the vertical groups of objects in an array.

The **array** of stars below has 3 **rows** and 4 **columns**. You can find the number of stars in the array by breaking apart the array into groups (rows or columns) and using addition strategies.

Break apart the array into 3 groups of 4 stars.
You can use a number sentence:
4 + 4 + 4 = 12
Or you can use skip counting by 4s:
4, 8, 12

Here is another way to count the number of stars.

Break apart the array into 4 groups of 3 stars.
You can use a number sentence:
3 + 3 + 3 + 3 = 12
Or you can use skip counting by 3s:
3, 6, 9, 12

Invite your child to share what he or she knows about arrays by doing the following activity together.

Arrays Activity

- With your child, look for arrays in and around your home.
  - Examples: floor or wall tiles, window panes, a carton of eggs, a pack of bottles or cans, a package of English muffins, plants in a garden, shoes on shelves, or arrays made with buttons, fruit, or coins.

- For each array, ask your child to say how he or she could split up the array into groups and the number of items in each group.
  - Example: For an egg carton, your child might say "2 groups of 6 eggs" or "6 groups of 2 eggs."

- Add to find out how many items there are in the array.
  - Example: 6 + 6 = 12 or 2 + 2 + 2 + 2 + 2 + 2 = 12

You can skip count by 2s to find the total number of eggs: 2, 4, 6, 8, 10, 12.

Add Using Arrays

Name: _____

Prerequisite: Add Three Numbers

Study the example showing adding three numbers. Then solve Problems 1–7.

Example

$3 + 2 + 4 = ?$

Add 2 numbers. $3 + 2 + 4 = ?$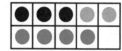

Add the third number. $5 \quad + 4 = 9$

$3 + 2 + 4 = 9$

---

1 Fill in the missing numbers to find $5 + 2 + 3$.

$5 \quad + 2 + 3 = \quad ?$

_____ + _____ = _____

2 Fill in the missing numbers to find $4 + 6 + 2$. Which numbers did you add first? Explain why.

$4 + 6 + 2 = \quad ?$

_____ + _____ = _____

_____

_____

_____

Solve.

3 Count up to complete each list. You can use the table.

1	2	3	4	5	6	7	8	9	10
11	12	13	14	15	16	17	18	19	20

  a. Count up by 2s.

     2, 4, _____, _____, _____

  b. Count up by 5s.

     5, 10, _____, _____

  c. Count up by 3s.

     3, 6, 9, _____, _____, _____

4 $2 + 2 + 2 =$ _____

5 $5 + 5 + 5 =$ _____

6 $6 + 6 + 6 =$ _____

7 Mell has 4 blue beads, 4 yellow beads, and 4 green beads. How many beads does she have in all?

Show your work.

Answer: _____

Name: _____

Add Using Arrays

Study the example showing two ways to find the number of shapes in an array. Then solve Problems 1–5.

Example

You can add to find the number of objects in an array.

Add the number of pears in each row.   Or   Add the number of pears in each column.

 2
 2
 2

2 + 2 + 2 = 6

3   3

3 + 3 = 6

There are 6 pears in all.

---

1. Write two number sentences you could use to find the total number of shapes in this array.

_____

_____

2. Use the columns in Problem 1. Show how you could skip count to find the total number of shapes.

_____

Vocabulary

array a set of objects grouped in equal rows and equal columns.

Solve.

3 Students line up in 3 rows for a relay race. There are 5 students in each row. How many students are in the race? Draw an array to show your answer.

Show your work.

Answer: _____

4 Look at your work in Problem 3. Suppose another group of 5 students join the race. Does the array change? Does the number sentence change? Explain.

_____

_____

_____

5 Lee makes 18 paper snowflakes to put on the wall. He wants to put them in an array of 4 rows and 4 columns. Does he make enough snowflakes? Explain.

_____

_____

_____

Name: _____

Add Using Arrays

Solve the problems.

1 Does the number sentence show the total number of leaves in the array?

Circle *Yes* or *No* for each.

How can you use the rows to write a number sentence? How can you use the columns?

a. $4 + 3 = 7$ Yes   No

b. $4 + 4 + 4 = 12$ Yes   No

c. $3 + 3 + 3 + 3 = 12$ Yes   No

d. $3 + 3 + 4 + 4 = 14$ Yes   No

2 Write two different ways you can skip-count to find the number of leaves in Problem 1.

How can you use the rows to skip count? The columns?

_____

3 An array has 3 rows with 3 items in each row. How many number sentences can you write to show the total? Explain.

Can you draw a picture to help?

_____

_____

_____

Solve.

4 Which sum describes the total number of squares in this array? Circle the correct answer.

A 2 + 2   **C** 3 + 3

B 2 + 3   **D** 3 + 3 + 3

Nikki chose **B** as the answer. This answer is wrong. How did Nikki get her answer?

_____

_____

_____

_____

_____

5 This picture shows a box filled with water bottles. They are packed in an array. Some of the bottles are covered by the lid.

How many water bottles could be in the box? Circle all correct answers.

A 9   **C** 16

B 12   **D** 18

Dear Family,

This week your child is learning to solve two-step word problems using models, and addition and subtraction number sentences.

---

two-step word problem: a word problem you need steps to solve.

Consider this word problem: There are 17 flowers in a vase. 8 flowers are daisies. 3 are roses. The rest are mums. How many are mums?

There are multiple ways to solve this two-step problem.

You could solve by first subtracting the number of daisies from the total number of flowers.
17 − 8 = 9

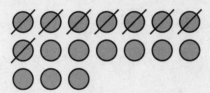

Then you subtract the number of roses.
9 − 3 = 6

There are 6 mums.

You could also solve the problem by adding the number of daisies and roses first and then subtracting that number from the total number of flowers.

8 + 3 = 11   17 − 11 = 6   There are 6 mums.

Invite your child to share what he or she knows about solving two-step word problems by doing the following activity together.

NEXT

Materials: paper and pencil, ingredients for a punch or snack mix (optional)

With your child, pretend you are making a snack mix and fruit punch for a party using the ingredients below. Ask your child to help you solve each word problem.

- You want to make 10 cups of snack mix. You have 4 cups of walnuts and 4 cups of raisins. How many cups of chocolate chips do you need?

- You need 6 cups of fruit punch. Use 2 cups of pineapple juice. Add 1 cup of cranberry juice. How many cups of orange juice should you add?

recipes

Snack Mix

Ingredients:
- Walnuts
- Raisins
- Chocolate Chips

recipes

Fruit Punch

Ingredients:
- Pineapple Juice
- Cranberry Juice
- Orange Juice

Solve Two-Step Word Problems

Name: _____

Study the example showing using a model to solve a word problem. Then solve Problems 1–5.

Example

Rex has 8 snails in a bucket. He finds more. Now he has 13 snails. How many more snails did Rex find?

Use a model. Write what you know.

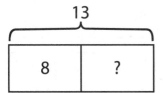

Write a number sentence. Solve.

$13 = 8 + ?$

$13 = 8 + 5$

Write the anwer: Rex found 5 more snails.

---

1. Some paintbrushes are in a jar. Jen takes out 4. Now there are 8 left. How many paintbrushes were in the jar to start?

   Show your work.

   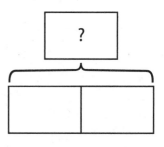

   Answer: _____

2. Compare the models in the Example and in Problem 1. Explain why the question mark (?) is in a different place in each.

   _____

   _____

Solve.

3 A pet store has 9 dog leashes. It has
8 fewer dog leashes than dog collars.
How many dog collars does the store
have?

Show your work.

Answer: _____

4 Write a problem that can be solved using
this tape diagram.

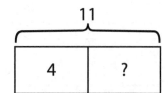

_____

_____

_____

_____

5 Show how to solve the problem you
wrote in Problem 4.

_____

_____

_____

_____

Name: _____

Use Tape Diagrams to Solve Two-Step Problems

Study the example showing one way to solve a two-step problem. Then solve Problems 1–4.

Example

There are 7 balls in the gym closet. Then 3 balls are taken out. After class, 9 balls are returned. How many balls are in the closet now?

Step 1   7 balls − 3 balls = 4 balls

Step 2   4 balls + 9 balls = **13** balls

Answer: There are 13 balls in the closet now.

7

3	4

4	9

13

---

1 Jay has 13 posters for the book fair. He hangs 5 in the morning. Then he hangs 4 more in the afternoon. How many posters does Jay have left?

Circle a number sentence for Step 1.

Underline a number sentence for Step 2.

$5 - 4 = 1$ $13 - 4 = 9$

$8 - 4 = 4$ $13 - 5 = 8$

2 Jay has _____ posters left.

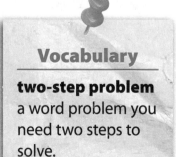

Vocabulary

two-step problem
a word problem you need two steps to solve.

Solve.

3 There are 15 people on a train. At the first stop 8 people get off the train and 3 people get on. How many people are on the train now?

Complete the tape diagrams.

Show your work.

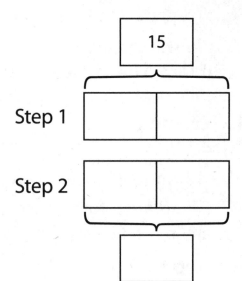

Answer: _____

_____

4 A box holds 12 markers. Nan takes out 6. Then she puts 2 back. Are there enough markers in the box for Fen to take out 10? Explain.

Show your work.

_____

_____

_____

Name: _____

Use Open Number Lines to Solve Two-Step Problems

Study the example showing one way to solve two-step problems. Then solve Problems 1–5.

Example

There are 8 apples and some bananas on the counter. Someone buys 3 apples. Now there are 4 more bananas than apples. How many bananas are there?

Step 1   8 apples − 3 apples

Step 2   There are 5 apples.
There are 4 more bananas than apples.

Answer: There are 9 bananas.

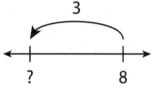

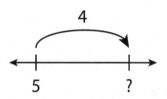

1. Look at the Example. Then complete the number sentences to show Step 1 and Step 2.

   Step 1   8 − _____ = _____

   Step 2   _____ + 4 = _____

2. Think about the Example. Could you do Step 2 first? Explain.

   _____

   _____

   _____

Solve.

3 There are 9 players on the field. Then 6 more players come to the field. They make two teams. There are 8 players on one team. How many are on the other team?

Show your work.

Answer: _____

4 Val has 11 bunnies in a pen. Then he sells 4 bunnies. Then some bunnies are born. Now there are 13 bunnies in the pen. How many bunnies are born?

Circle the correct answer.

A 6   **C** 8

B 7   **D** 9

5 Look at Problem 4. If Val has 14 bunnies at the end instead of 13 bunnies, would Step 1 change? Would Step 2 change? Explain.

_____

_____

_____

Name: _____

Solve Two-Step Word Problems

Solve the problems.

1 There are 18 ducks in the pond. First 9 ducks fly away. Then 3 more ducks fly away. How many ducks are in the pond now? Circle the correct answer.

What do the ducks do in Step 1? In Step 2?

A 3   **C** 9

B 6   **D** 12

2 Will has 8 stickers. He gives 2 to Sara. Then he puts some on his lunch bag. He has 4 stickers left. How many does he put on his lunch bag? Circle the correct answer.

Does Will have more or fewer stickers after he gives 2 to Sara?

A 2   **C** 6

B 4   **D** 10

Sam chose **D**. This answer is wrong. How did Sam get her answer?

_____

_____

_____

_____

_____

Solve.

3 Sal has 8 balloons. He has 3 red balloons. The rest are blue. Kay has 5 more blue balloons than Sal. How many blue balloons does Kay have? Circle the correct answer.

What do you need to find in Step 1?

A 5

B 8

C 10

D 16

4 Choose a number sentence.

$3 + 8 = 11$ $2 + 5 = 7$
$15 - 6 = 9$ $9 - 4 = 5$

Write a two-step word problem. Your number sentence must be used to solve one of the steps.

What are some actions that you would use plus or minus for?

_____

_____

_____

_____

_____

_____

Unit 1 Game

Model Match!

What you need: Recording Sheet, Number Sentence Cards, Model Cards

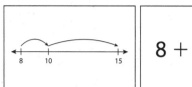

Directions

- Mix up the Model Cards. Place them face down in a pile.

- Mix up the Number Sentence Cards. Place them face down in a different pile. Each player takes 3 Number Sentence Cards.

- One player flips the top Model Card. If the model shows a number sentence held by either player, that player wins that pair of cards.

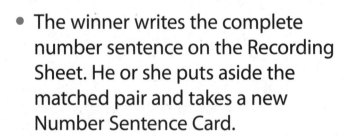

- The winner writes the complete number sentence on the Recording Sheet. He or she puts aside the matched pair and takes a new Number Sentence Card.

- If there is no match, put that Model Card on the bottom of the pile.

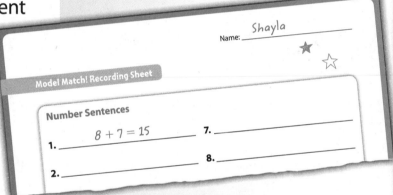

I got a match! I used the model to help me complete the number sentence.

- Take turns flipping a Model Card. Play until all the Model Cards are gone. The player with the most matches wins the game.

Model Match! Recording Sheet

Number Sentences

1. _____ 7. _____

2. _____ 8. _____

3. _____ 9. _____

4. _____ 10. _____

5. _____ 11. _____

6. _____ 12. _____

I played with _____.

His/Her final score was: [   ]

My final score was: [   ]

$$12 - 7 = \square$$

$$\square - 7 = 9$$

$$8 + 7 = \square$$

$$12 - 9 = \square$$

$$13 - 5 = \square$$

$$14 - \square = 8$$

$$\square - 6 = 9$$

$$8 + \square = 16$$

$\square + 8 = 11$

$7 + 7 = \square$

$9 + \square = 11$

$9 + 5 = \square$

$9 + \square = 18$

$10 - \square = 6$

$\square + 8 = 17$

$13 - 9 = \square$

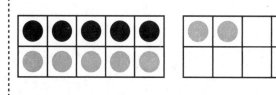

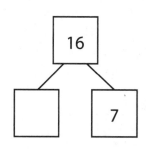

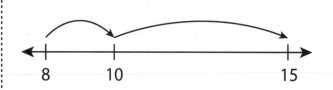

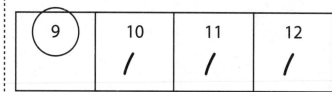

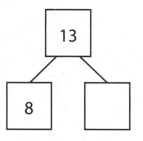

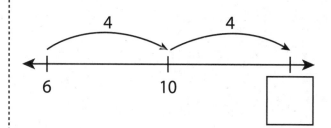

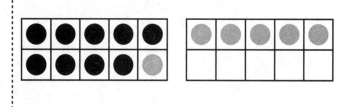

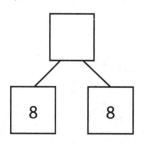

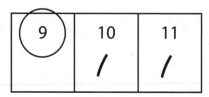

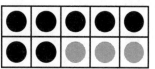

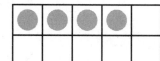

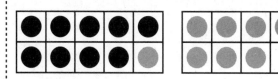

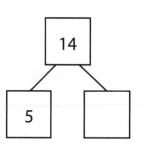

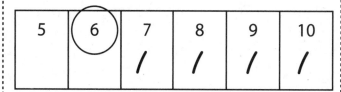

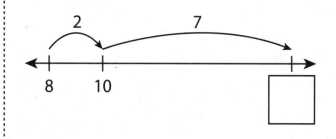

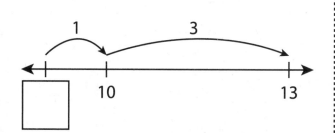

Unit 1 Operations and Algebraic Thinking   **61**

Unit 1 Practice

Operations and Algebraic Thinking

In this unit you learned to:	Lesson
use fact families to add and subtract.	1
count on to add and subtract.	1
add two numbers by finding the sum of 10 first.	3
solve a one-step word problem.	2
find even and odd numbers.	4
use addition to find the total number of objects in an array.	5
use addition and subtraction to solve a problem with more than one step.	6

Use these skills to solve Problems 1–5.

1 Show how to solve 12 − 5 with both models.

12

5

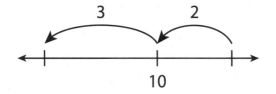

3   2

10

12 − 5 = _____

2 How can you skip count to find the total number of rectangles?
Circle all the correct answers.

A 3, 6, 9, 12, 15

B 5, 10, 15

C 3, 6, 9, 12

D 5, 10, 15, 20

Solve.

3 Myra has 14 beads. There are 6 white beads. The rest are green. How many green beads does Myra have?

Use the tape diagram to show the problem. Then write two number sentences.

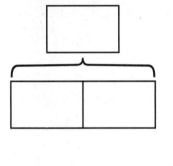

_____ − _____ = _____

_____ = _____ + _____

Answer: _____

4 Write two different number sentences to show the number of triangles in this array. Is the total an odd or even number? Tell how you know.

▲ ▲
▲ ▲
▲ ▲
▲ ▲
▲ ▲

Show your work.

_____

_____

_____

_____

_____

5 Tara has 7 points. She gets 6 more on her next turn. On her last turn, she loses points. She ends with 9 points. How many points did Tara lose on her last turn?

Show your work.

Answer: _____

Name: _____

Answer the questions and show all your work on separate paper.

You are buying balloons for a party. This is what you know:

- You can buy no more than 20 balloons.

- You will put the same number of balloons inside and outside.

- You will put some of the inside balloons in the kitchen and some in the living room.

Make a plan that shows how many balloons you will buy and how many you will put in each place. Tell why your numbers work.

Use the tools on the back of this page.

- Make a table to show how many balloons you need.

- Write a number sentence to show that the number of balloons inside equals the number of balloons outside.

- Use the sentence starters to help you tell why your numbers work.

Reflect on Mathematical Practices

Make Sense of Problems How did you decide the number of balloons to put inside and outside?

Checklist

Did you . . .
- ☐ make a chart?
- ☐ make sure your numbers fit the plan?
- ☐ tell why your numbers work?

Performance Task Tips

Word Bank Here are some words that you might use in your answer.

equal	sum	total
same	number	compare
more	fewer	

Models Here are some models and tools that you can use to find a solution.

Place	Number of Balloons
Living Room	?
Kitchen	?
Outside	?

TOTAL: _____

balloons in kitchen + balloons in living room = balloons outside

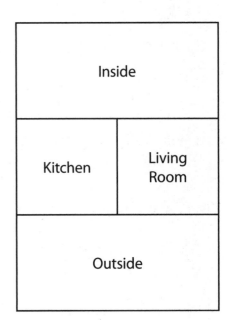

Sentence Starters Here are some sentence starters that can help you explain your work.

The total number of balloons is _____

The total number of balloons inside _____

The total number of balloons outside _____

Unit 1 Vocabulary

Name: _____

My Examples

fact family

a group of facts that all use the same three numbers

one-step problem

a word problem you can solve with one step

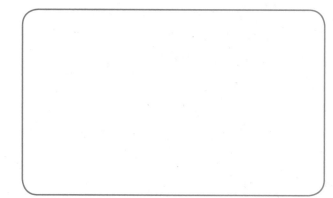

two-step problem

a word problem you need two steps to solve

array

a set of objects grouped in equal rows and equal columns

My Examples

column

a top-to-bottom group of objects in an array

row

a side-to-side group of objects in an array

even number

an even number of objects can be put into pairs

odd number

an odd number of objects cannot be put into pairs

68 Unit 1 Vocabulary ©Curriculum Associates, LLC Copying is not permitted.

My Words

My Examples

My Words

My Examples

_____

_____

_____

_____

_____

_____

_____

_____

_____

_____

_____

_____

Dear Family,

This week your child is learning to use different strategies to add two-digit numbers.

Here are some ways to find the sum 28 + 47.

Use base-ten blocks.

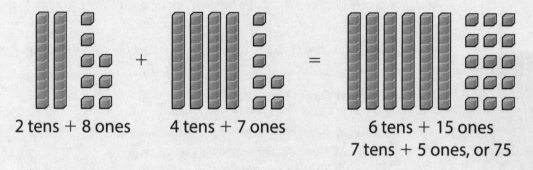

2 tens + 8 ones   4 tens + 7 ones   6 tens + 15 ones
7 tens + 5 ones, or 75

Add tens and ones.

$28 = 20 + 8$
$47 = \underline{40 + 7}$
$60 + 15 = 75$

Go on to the next 10.

It is easier to add when one number has no ones. To simplify adding, go on to the next ten.

$28 + \mathbf{2} = 30$
$30 + \mathbf{40} = 70$
$70 + \mathbf{5} = 75$
$28 + 47 = 75$

Invite your child to share what he or she knows about addition strategies by doing the following activity together.

Addition Strategies Activity

Materials: 2 number cubes, pencil and paper

- Explain to your child that the point of the game is to get a sum greater than 75.

- Have your child roll two number cubes.

- Ask your child to form a two-digit number from the number cubes (For example, if you roll a 2 and a 6 you can make 26 or 62.) Write the number down.

- Ask your child to add 25 to the number, using one of the addition strategies shown on the other side of this paper.

- If the sum is greater than 75, then he or she wins the round. Repeat the game 3 more times.

- Ask your child questions during the game.
  - Example:
    - Does it matter which number you make with the two number cubes? Will you get the same sum either way?
    - How can you pick the numbers to make sure your sum is as large as possible?

Will my two-digit number be greater if I use the larger digit in the tens place or the ones place?

Add Two-Digit Numbers

Name: _____

Study the example showing how to add two-digit numbers. Then solve Problems 1–8.

Example

Sid has 32 marbles. Nan has 16 marbles. How many do they have altogether?

Write 32 and 16 as tens and ones: 3 tens 2 ones and 1 ten 6 ones.

Add the tens first. Then add the ones. → 32 marbles

$$
\begin{array}{ll}
 & 3 \text{ tens} \quad 2 \text{ ones} \\
+ & 1 \text{ ten} \quad\ \, 6 \text{ ones} \\
\hline
 & 4 \text{ tens} \quad 8 \text{ ones} = \mathbf{48}
\end{array}
$$

→ 16 marbles
48 marbles

Mark has 43 shells. Then he finds 25 more shells.

1 There are _____ tens and _____ ones in 43.

2 There are _____ tens and _____ ones in 25.

3 How many shells does Mark have now?

Show your work.

Answer: Mark has _____ shells.

Solve.

Leah has 33 heart stickers. She has 16 star stickers.

4 Circle groups of ten heart stickers.

There are _____ tens and _____ ones in 33.

5 Write the tens and the ones for the heart stickers in the number bond.

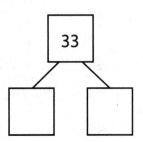

6 Circle a group of ten star stickers.

There are _____ ten and _____ ones in 16.

7 Write the tens and the ones for the star stickers in the number bond.

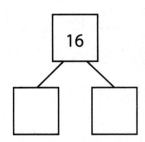

8 How many stickers does Leah have in all?

Show your work.

Answer: Leah has _____ stickers in all.

Name: _____

Use Base-Ten Blocks to Add Two-Digit Numbers

Study the example showing how to use base-ten blocks to add two-digit numbers. Then solve Problems 1–7.

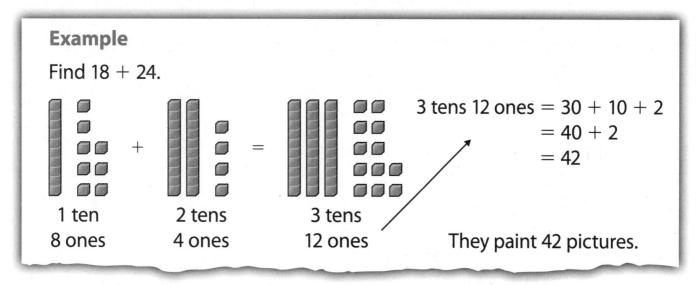

Example

Find $18 + 24$.

1 ten 8 ones $+$ 2 tens 4 ones $=$ 3 tens 12 ones

3 tens 12 ones $= 30 + 10 + 2$
$= 40 + 2$
$= 42$

They paint 42 pictures.

Max has 29 rocks. Then he finds 15 more rocks.

1 Write the tens and ones. Then add the tens and ones.

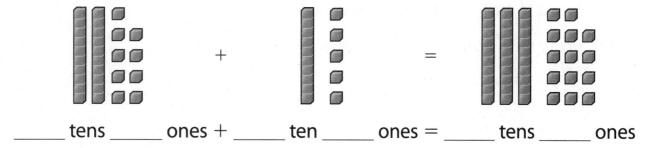

_____ tens _____ ones + _____ ten _____ ones = _____ tens _____ ones

2 How many tens and ones are in 14?

$14 = $ _____ ten and _____ ones, or $10 + $ _____

3 Add the tens. Then add the ones.

$30 + 10 + 4 = $ _____ + _____ , or _____

Max has _____ rocks.

Solve.

> Ms. Kottler has 27 black pens and 14 blue pens.

4   Write the tens and ones.

27 = 20 + __7__

14 = __10__ + __4__

5   Add the tens then add the ones from Problem 4. How many pens does Ms. Kottler have in all?

Show your work.

$$20 + 7$$
$$10 + 4$$
$$\overline{30 \quad 11}$$
$$3 + (0 +) = 41$$

Answer: __41__ pens

> There are 36 girls with red shirts. There are 19 boys with red shirts. There are 16 girls with blue shirts.

6   How many girls are there?

Show your work.

$$30 + 6$$
$$10 + 9$$
$$\overline{40 \quad 15}$$
$$40 + 10 + 5 = 55$$

Answer: __52__ girls

7   How many children have red shirts?

Show your work.

$$30 + 6$$
$$10 + 9$$
$$\overline{40 \quad 15}$$
$$40 + 10 + 5 = 55$$

Answer: __55__ red shirts

Name: _____

Use Quick Drawings or Open Number Lines to Add Two-Digit Numbers

Study the example showing how to use quick drawings to add two-digit numbers. Then solve Problems 1–6.

Example

What is $37 + 24$?

$37 + 24$ is the same as $40 + 21$.

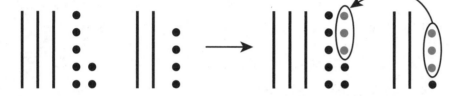

$40 + 21 = 61$

So, $37 + 24 = 61$

Kim picks 28 apples. Nate picks 17 apples.

1 Look at the quick drawing. Then fill in the blanks.

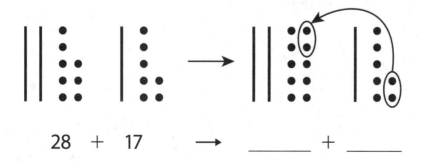

28 + 17 → _____ + _____

2 How many apples do Kim and Nate pick in all? _____

Lesson 7 Add Two-Digit Numbers   **77**

Solve.

3 57 + 14 is the same as _____ + _____ .

4 Fill in the missing numbers in the open number line. Then solve 57 + 14.

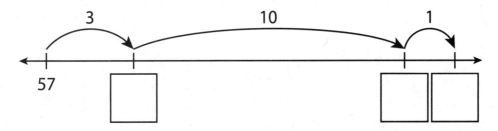

57 + 14 = _____

5 Mia has 49 red beads and 36 yellow beads. How many beads does Mia have in all?

Show your work.

Answer: _____

6 Write three different number sentences with a sum of 51.

22 + 29 = 51

_____

_____

_____

Name: _____

Add Two-Digit Numbers

Solve the problems.

1 Diego read 48 pages of a book one day. The next day he read 23 pages. How many pages did Diego read in all? Circle the correct answer.

You can add the tens and add the ones.

A 61   **C** 71

B 62   **D** 75

2 Which addition problems could be solved by adding 40 + 15? Circle all of the correct answers.

What do you add to one of the addends to get 40?

A 39 + 16   **C** 37 + 18

B 38 + 13   **D** 36 + 17

3 Tell if the number sentence can be used to solve 27 + 56. Circle *Yes* or *No* for each number sentence.

There are many ways to add two-digit numbers.

a. 20 + 50 + 10 + 6 = 86   Yes   No

b. 20 + 7 + 50 + 6 = 83   Yes   No

c. 30 + 56 = 86   Yes   No

d. 20 + 50 + 13 = 83   Yes   No

Solve.

4　A fruit salad has 37 green grapes and 45 red grapes. How many grapes are in the fruit salad?

A 72　　　　　**C** 82

B 81　　　　　**D** 712

Tim chose **A**. This is wrong. How did Tim get his answer?

How many tens are you adding?

_____

_____

_____

_____

5　Dan has 29 books. Kayla has 3 more books than Dan. How many books do Dan and Kayla have altogether?

Show your work.

How many books does Kayla have?

Answer: _____

Dear Family,

This week your child is learning strategies for subtracting two-digit numbers.

Consider the following problem: Rex has 65 dollars. He spends 37 dollars. How much money does he have left?

One strategy is called "adding up."
The subtraction sentence $65 - 37 = ?$ is the same as the addition sentence $37 + ? = 65$. How much do you have to add to 37 to get to 65? Here's one way to think about it.

$37 + \mathbf{20} = 57$
$57 + \mathbf{3} = 60$
$60 + \mathbf{5} = 65$
$\mathbf{20 + 3 + 5 = 28}$

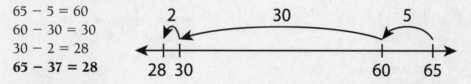

So, $37 + 28 = 65$, and $65 - 37 = 28$.

Another strategy is called "subtracting to make a ten."
65 has 5 ones, so you can just subtract 5 first. Then subtract the tens. Then subtract the rest of the ones.

$65 - 5 = 60$
$60 - 30 = 30$
$30 - 2 = 28$
$\mathbf{65 - 37 = 28}$

Whichever method you choose to use, you will get the same answer: Rex has 28 dollars left.

Invite your child to share what he or she knows about subtracting by doing the following activity together.

Subtracting Activity

Make up a subtraction word problem using two-digit numbers you encounter in your everyday life. Use ideas like these:

- Our dog weighs 27 pounds. The cat weighs 12 pounds. How much more does the dog weigh?

- Your brother has saved 21 dollars. How much more does he need so he can buy that 49-dollar video game he's been wanting?

- It is 65 miles from home to Grandma's house, and 78 miles from home to the amusement park. How much farther is it to the park than to Grandma's house?

- The chapter book we are reading has 84 pages. We have read 55 pages. How many more pages do we have to read?

Have your child write and solve a number sentence and then draw a picture to illustrate the word problem.

You can also use a bar model or a tape diagram to help you solve subtraction problems.

Subtract Two-Digit Numbers

Prerequisite: Subtract Tens

Study the example showing how to subtract tens. Then solve Problems 1–5.

Example

$50 - 20 = ?$ is the same as $20 + ? = 50$

Write as tens.
2 tens + ? tens = 5 tens
2 tens + 3 tens = 5 tens
$20 + 30 = 50$

$50 - 20 = 30$

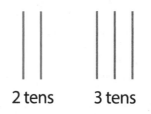

2 tens   3 tens

John has 60 white and red balloons. There are 40 white balloons.

1 Fill in the blanks.

$40 + ? = $ _____

4 tens + _____ tens = _____ tens

$40 + $ _____ $ = 60$

$60 - 40 = $ _____

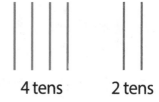

4 tens   2 tens

2 How many balloons are red? _____

Solve.

3 Mr. Lin has 80 rubber bands. He puts 30 of the rubber bands in a drawer. The rest are on the table. How many rubber bands are on the table?

Show your work.

Answer: There are _____ rubber bands on the table.

4 Jada has 70 pens. She gives away 50 pens. How many pens are left?

Show your work.

Answer: _____

5 Marco and Jess fold 60 napkins altogether. Jess folds 20 more napkins than Marco. How many napkins do they each fold?

Show your work.

Answer: _____

_____

Subtract Two-Digit Numbers by Adding Up

Study the example that shows how to subtract two-digit numbers by adding up. Then solve Problems 1–6.

Example

A store has 82 hats. There are 45 blue hats. The rest are red. How many hats are red?

$82 - 45 = \boxed{?}$ is the same as $45 + \boxed{?} = 82$.

You can add tens first. Then add ones.

$45 + 30 = 75$
$75 + 5 = 80$
$80 + 2 = 82$

$30 + 5 + 2 = 37$. There are 37 red hats in the store.

Mr. Kent needs 74 plates for a picnic. He has 28 plates. He will buy the rest of the plates he needs.

1 Show how you can find how many plates Mr. Kent needs to buy. Fill in the blanks to find $74 - 28$. Add tens first.

$28 + \underline{\hspace{1cm}} = 68$

$68 + \underline{\hspace{1cm}} = 70$

$70 + \underline{\hspace{1cm}} = 74$

$40 + \underline{\hspace{1cm}} + \underline{\hspace{1cm}} = \underline{\hspace{1cm}}$

2 How many plates should Mr. Kent buy?

_____ plates

Solve.

Ms. Jones has 54 pencils. She gives 17 of the pencils to her students.

3 Show how you can add ones first to find 54 − 17. Fill in the blanks on the number line.

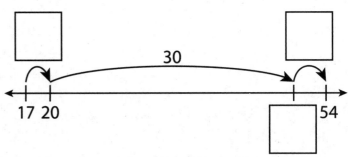

4 How many pencils does Ms. Jones have left?

Show your work.

_____ pencils

There are 65 trees in the town park. 38 are apple trees. The rest are oak trees.

5 How many oak trees are there? Add up to find 65 − 38.

Show your work.

Answer: _____

6 To solve Problem 5, did you add tens or ones first? Explain why.

_____

_____

Name: _____

Subtract Two-Digit Numbers by Regrouping

Study the example showing how to subtract two-digit numbers by regrouping a ten. Then solve Problems 1–6.

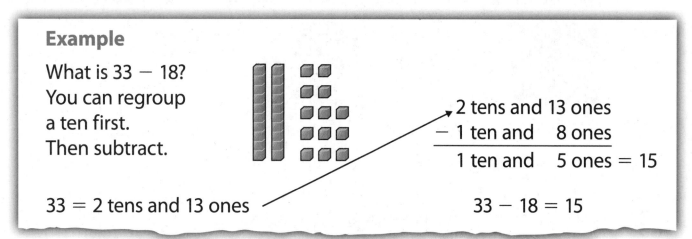

Example

What is 33 − 18?
You can regroup
a ten first.
Then subtract.

33 = 2 tens and 13 ones

 2 tens and 13 ones
− 1 ten and   8 ones
——————————————
 1 ten and   5 ones = 15

33 − 18 = 15

Kate paints 44 stars. She paints 27 of the stars silver. She paints the rest gold.

1 Regroup a ten in 44. Fill in the blank.

44 = 3 tens and _____ ones

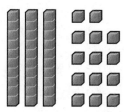

2 How many stars are gold? Find 44 − 27.
Show your work.

Answer: _____ stars are gold.

Solve.

3 Subtract tens first to solve 51 − 22. Fill in the blanks.

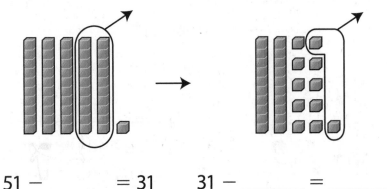

51 − _____ = 31   31 − _____ = _____

4 Wyatt solved 57 − 38. He subtracted tens first. Fill in the blanks to show the next step and the answer.

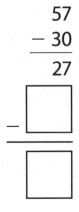

5 There are 32 boys and girls on the playground. There are 19 girls. How many boys are on the playground?

Show your work.

Answer: _____

6 This is how Dora subtracts 73 − 26. Fill in the blanks to finish the problem.

73 − 3 = _____

70 − _____ = 50

_____ − _____ = _____

Name: _____

Subtract Two-Digit Numbers

Solve the problems.

1 There are 54 children in a parade. 15 hold flags. The rest play instruments. How many children play instruments? Find 54 − 15.

Show your work.

Answer: _____

2 Show another way to find 54 − 15. Make sure it is different than what you did in Problem 1.

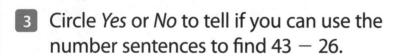

You can regroup a ten first. You can also subtract tens first.

3 Circle *Yes* or *No* to tell if you can use the number sentences to find 43 − 26.

How many tens and ones are in 26?

a. 26 + 4 = 30 and
30 + 13 = 43   Yes   No

b. 26 + 10 = 36 and
36 + 3 = 39   Yes   No

c. 43 − 10 = 33 and
33 − 6 = 27   Yes   No

d. 43 − 20 = 23 and
23 − 6 = 17   Yes   No

Solve.

4 There are 86 cars in the parking lot. Then 37 cars drive away. How many cars are in the parking lot now? Find 86 − 37. Circle the correct answer.

How can you write 86 so that you have 16 ones?

A 59   **C** 49

B 58   **D** 48

Lin chose **A**. This is wrong. How did Lin get her answer?

_____

_____

_____

5 How can you find 72 − 25? Circle all the correct answers.

What methods do you know for subtracting two-digit numbers?

A 72 − 30 = 42 and
42 − 5 = 37

B 25 + 5 = 30 and
30 + 40 = 70 and
70 + 2 = 72

C
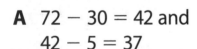
40   5 2

25   65   70 72

D   6 tens   12 ones
      − 2 tens   5 ones

Dear Family,

This week your child is learning to solve one-step problems by adding and subtracting two-digit numbers.

A one-step problem requires a single step to solve. You can think about one-step addition problems as:

- Start with a number.

- Change happens.

- Get a total.

This can be modeled different ways to help your child write and solve number sentences.

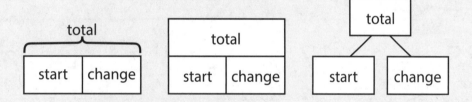

Consider this word problem: Jacinda had 15 pieces of sea glass in her collection. She went to the beach and collected some more, and now she has 32 pieces of sea glass. How many pieces of sea glass did she collect?

32	
15	?

$15 + ? = 32$
$32 - 15 = ?$
$32 - 15 = 17$

Jacinda collected 17 pieces of sea glass.

Invite your child to share what he or she knows about solving one-step problems by doing the following activity together.

Lesson 9 Solve One-Step Word Problems With Two-Digit Numbers

Solving One-Step Word Problems With Two-Digit Numbers Activity

Materials: pen and paper, scissors (optional)

- Help your child to create word problem cards, by cutting out the prompts below or writing the prompts on index cards.

- Ask your child to pick two numbers and one category card.

- Ask your child to come up with an addition or subtraction word problem involving the numbers and category. (If your child chose 25, 42, and *dollars*, he or she might say "Mike had 42 dollars and earned 25 more dollars. How much money does he have now?")

- Ask your child to solve the word problem.

- Work with your child to create and solve 5 more word problems, picking combinations of numbers and categories each time.

38	17	Books	Dollars
29	40	Apples	Balls
16	25	Seashells	Pennies
42	11	Pencils	People

Solve One-Step Word Problems With Two-Digit Numbers

Name: _____

Study the example showing how to solve a word problem. Then solve Problems 1–7.

Example

Seth had 8 toy cars. Then his friend gave him more cars. Now Seth has 12 cars. How many cars did Seth's friend give him?

Use a model.

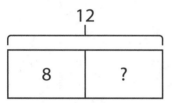

Use a number sentence.

$8 + ? = 12$ or $12 - 8 = ?$ or $12 - ? = 8$

Seth's friend gave him 4 cars.

There are 17 students in the gym. There are 9 boys.

1 What number is the total? What part do you know? Complete the tape diagram.

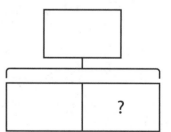

2 Complete the number sentences.

_____ $+ ? = 17$ $17 -$ _____ $= ?$

$17 - ? =$ _____

3 How many girls are in the gym? _____

   Lesson 9 Solve One-Step Word Problems With Two-Digit Numbers   **93**

Solve.

There are 7 birds on a fence. More birds join them. Then there are 13 birds on the fence.

4 How many birds joined the 7 on the fence? Write three number sentences you could use to solve.

_____ + ? = _____

_____ − ? = _____

_____ − _____ = ?

5 How many birds joined the first 7 birds?

_____

Ryan had 6 acorns and Jo had 15 acorns. Then Jo gives Ryan some acorns. Now Ryan has 11 acorns.

6 How many acorns do Ryan and Jo have altogether?

Show your work.

Answer: _____

7 How many acorns did Jo give Ryan?

Show your work.

Answer: _____

Use Number Sentences to Solve Word Problems

Study the example showing how to use number sentences to solve word problems. Then solve Problems 1–6.

Example

Ted has some beads. Then he gets 18 more beads. Now Ted has 42 beads. How many beads did Ted have to begin with?

42	
?	18

Use addition: or   Use subtraction:
start + change = total   total − change = start
  ? + 18   = 42   42 − 18   = ?

? = 24

Ted had 24 beads to begin with.

Mrs. Tate has some fish in her fish tank. She buys 25 more fish. Now there are 73 fish in the fish tank.

1 Fill in the empty boxes of the model. Then complete the number sentences.

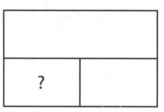

? + _____ = _____

_____ − _____ = ?

2 How many fish were in the fish tank at the start?

Show your work.

Answer: _____

Solve.

Mrs. Lopez drives a number of miles north.
Then she drives 34 miles west. She drives
93 miles in all.

3 Complete the number sentences to show
how many miles Mrs. Lopez drives north.

? + _____ = _____ and _____ − _____ = ?

4 Complete the open number line. Then
solve the problem.

Show your work.

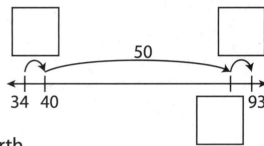

Answer: Mrs. Lopez drives _____ miles north.

Stella had some cards. Then she made
13 more cards. Now she has 41 cards.

5 How many cards did Stella start with?

Show your work.

Answer: _____

6 Write and solve a problem like Problem 5.
Use different numbers.

_____

_____

_____

Name: _____

Use Words and Numbers to Model Problems

Study the example showing how to model with words and numbers. Then solve Problems 1–6.

Example

Some ducks were in the pond. Then 17 flew away. Now there are 45 ducks in the pond. How many ducks were in the pond at the start?

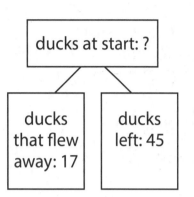

Model the problem with words or with numbers. Then write a number sentence.

$$17 + 45 = 62$$

There were 62 ducks to begin with.

Rick has some grapes. Rick eats 15 of the grapes. Then he has 19 grapes left.

1 Complete the number bond to model the problem.

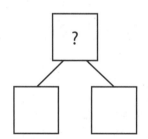

2 How many grapes did Rick start with?

Show your work.

Answer: _____

Solve.

A sports store sells baseball bats. In one week, 34 bats are sold. Then the store has 46 bats left. How many bats did the store have to begin with?

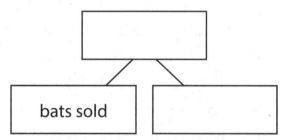

3 Model the problem with words. Complete the number bond.

4 Solve the problem.
Show your work.

Answer: _____

There were 41 people waiting at a bus stop. Then 23 of them got on a bus. Now there are 39 people on the bus.

5 Now how many people are still waiting at the bus stop?
Show your work.

Answer: _____

6 How many people were on the bus to begin with?
Show your work.

Answer: _____

Name: _____

Model and Solve Word Problems

Solve the problems.

1 Carlos sells 32 muffins at a bake sale. Jake sells 25 fewer muffins. How many muffins does Jake sell?

Who sells more muffins?

Which number sentences can you use to solve the problem? Circle *Yes* or *No* for each number sentence.

a. $25 + ? = 32$ Yes No

b. $25 + 32 = ?$ Yes No

c. $32 - ? = 25$ Yes No

d. $32 - 25 = ?$ Yes No

2 Some beads were in a box. Anne used 17 of them. Then there were 56 beads in the box. How many beads were in the box to begin with? Circle the correct answer.

Can you draw a model to help you think about the problem?

A 79

B 73

C 39

D 29

Dave chose **C**. This is wrong. How did Dave get his answer?

_____

_____

Solve.

3 The table shows how many roses of each color a store has for sale.

Red roses	65
Yellow roses	43
White roses	17

How many more red roses are there than white roses?

Show your work.

Can you write an addition sentence? Can you write a subtraction sentence?

Answer: _____

4 The store has 43 yellow roses. Chen buys some yellow roses. Then the store has 29 yellow roses left. How many yellow roses does Chen buy? Circle the correct answer.

What do you know? What are you trying to find out?

A 12   **C** 36

B 14   **D** 72

5 There are 23 solid shirts and 18 striped shirts on a rack. How many shirts are on the rack? Circle the correct answer.

Do you add or subtract to solve the problem?

A 5   **C** 41

B 15   **D** 43

Dear Family,

This week your child is exploring three-digit numbers.

The first three-digit number is 100. It is the same as 100 ones, 10 tens, or 1 hundred.

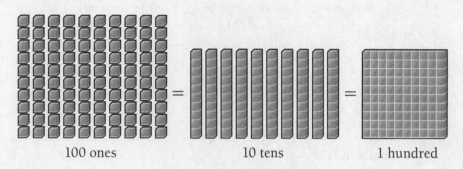

100 ones = 10 tens = 1 hundred

Three-digit numbers have a hundreds place, a tens place, and a ones place.

387

Hundreds	Tens	Ones
3	8	7

The hundreds place tells how many hundreds are in the number, the tens place tells how many tens, and the ones place tells how many ones.

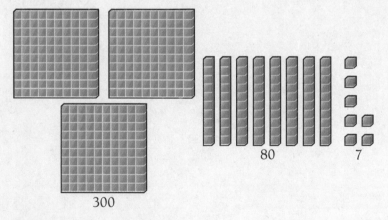

300   80   7

Invite your child to explain what he or she knows about three-digit numbers by doing the following activity together.

NEXT →

Hundreds Activity

Play the Guess My Number game.

- Think of a three-digit number (Example: 592).

- Give your child a clue and then have your child guess the number. The first clue should be which number is in the hundreds place. (Example: "5 is in the hundreds place.")

- If your child guesses your number, he or she wins the game. If the guess is incorrect, give your child another clue, the number in the tens place. (Example: "9 is in the tens place.")

- Have your child guess the number again. If the guess is incorrect give the final clue, the number in the ones place. (Example: "2 is in the ones place.")

- Encourage your child to use a place value chart to keep track of the clues and write the number.

Hundreds	Tens	Ones
5	9	2

- Play the game again and have your child pick the number and give the clues.

Name: _____

Prerequisite: **How are two-digit numbers made up of tens and ones?**

Study the example showing two-digit numbers as tens and ones. Then solve Problems 1–7.

Example

You can show 52 as tens and ones. You can show this in different ways.

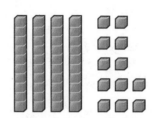

5 tens 2 ones
50 + 2 = 52

4 tens 12 ones
40 + 12 = 52

1 Show 36 as tens and ones. Fill in the blanks to show different ways.

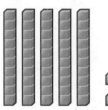
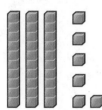

_____ tens _____ ones   _____ tens _____ ones

2 You can show tens and ones in a chart.
Complete the chart to show tens and ones in 36.

Tens	Ones
3	

3 Show tens and ones in 36 in a different way.
Complete the chart.

Tens	Ones

©Curriculum Associates, LLC   Copying is not permitted.

Lesson 10 Understand Three-Digit Numbers **103**

Solve.

4 What are two different ways 47 can be shown with tens and ones? Fill in the blanks.

_____ tens   _____ ones

_____ tens   _____ ones

5 What are three different ways 91 can be shown with tens and ones? Fill in the blanks.

_____ tens   _____ ones

_____ tens   _____ ones

_____ tens   _____ ones

6 What are two different ways 83 can be shown with tens and ones? Complete the charts.

Tens	Ones

Tens	Ones

7 Circle all the ways that show 54. Then write three other ways to show 54.

4 tens 14 ones   5 tens 4 ones

50 + 4   40 + 5

5 tens 14 ones   1 ten 44 ones

_____

_____

_____

Name: _____

Understand Hundreds, Tens, and Ones

Study the example showing how to count hundreds, tens, and ones. Then solve Problems 1–6.

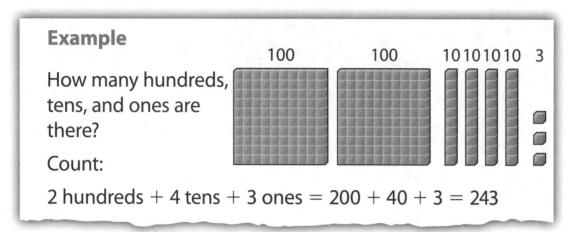

Example

How many hundreds, tens, and ones are there?

Count:

2 hundreds + 4 tens + 3 ones = 200 + 40 + 3 = 243

---

1 How many hundreds, tens, and ones are there?

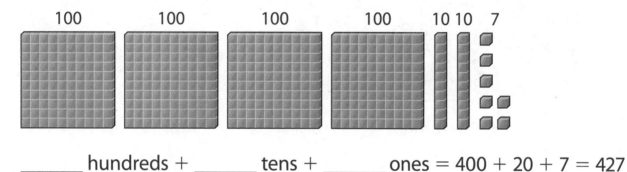

_____ hundreds + _____ tens + _____ ones = 400 + 20 + 7 = 427

---

2 How many hundreds, tens, and ones are there?

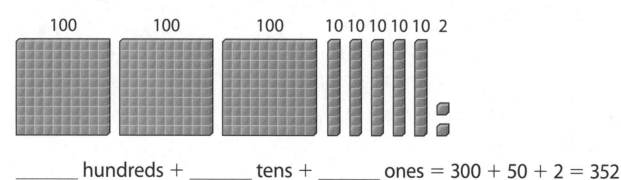

_____ hundreds + _____ tens + _____ ones = 300 + 50 + 2 = 352

Solve.

3 This model shows 200 in tens. How many tens are in 200?

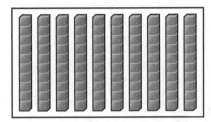

200 = _____ tens

4 This model shows 136 in tens. How many tens are in 136? How many ones are left over?

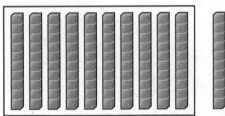 

136 = _____ tens and _____ ones

5 Complete the chart to show 7 hundreds + 5 ones.

Hundreds	Tens	Ones
	0	5

6 Complete the chart to show 9 hundreds + 4 tens + 8 ones.

Hundreds	Tens	Ones

Name: _____

Reason and Write

Look at the example. Underline a part that you think makes it a good answer.

Example

Eva uses her blocks to build towers of 10 blocks each. There are 15 towers and 2 blocks left over.

1. Draw a picture to show Eva's blocks. Write the total number of blocks that Eva has.

2. Explain how you figured out how many blocks Eva has.

3. Show a different way you can write how many blocks Eva has.

Draw.

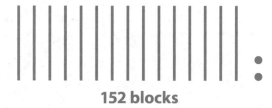

152 blocks

Explain.

First I counted 10 towers because 10 tens is 100 blocks. Then I counted 5 more towers. That is the same as 50. Then I saw that there were 2 blocks left over. So Eva has 100 + 50 + 2, or 152 blocks.

Show a different way.

1 hundred + 5 tens + 2 ones

Where does the example . . .

• show the picture?

• show the number of blocks?

• use words to explain?

• show a different way to write the number of blocks?

Solve the problem. Use what you learned from the example.

Ty uses his blocks to build towers of 10 blocks each. There are 14 towers and 5 blocks left over.

1. Draw a picture to show Ty's blocks. Write the total number of blocks that Ty has.

2. Explain how you figured out how many blocks Ty has.

3. Show a different way you can write how many blocks Ty has.

Did you . . .
• draw the picture?
• write the number of blocks?
• use words to explain?
• show a different way to write the number of blocks?

Draw.

Explain.

_____

_____

_____

Show a different way.

_____

Dear Family,

This week your child is learning to read and write three-digit numbers.

A **digit** is any one of the symbols we use to write numbers: 0, 1, 2, 3, 4, 5, 6, 7, 8, and 9. So a three-digit number is a number such as 153 or 201 or 999.

All numbers can be represented in different ways. These different ways each show something about what the number means.

You can write the number 279 many different ways.

You can write it as a sum of hundreds, tens, and ones:
200 + 70 + 9

You can use words:
two hundred seventy-nine

You can use a model or chart:

Hundreds	Tens	Ones
2	7	9

2 7 9

Invite your child to share what he or she knows about three-digit numbers by doing the following activity together.

- Give your child 2 or 3 three-digit numbers from your everyday life.
  - Examples:
    - Our neighbor's dog weighs 112 pounds.
    - The book Mom is reading has 437 pages.
    - The monthly rent is 875 dollars.
    - Your cousins live 268 miles away.

- Have your child write each number as a numeral and as a sum of hundreds, tens, and ones. For example, 279 is a numeral and it can be written as 200 + 70 + 9.

- Then, let your child make up 2 or 3 three-digit numbers for you to write.

- Ask your child to check your work.

- Alternatively, if you and your child are feeling imaginative, make up a short story together that includes two or three 3-digit numbers. Each of you can write the numbers as numerals and as sums of hundreds, tens, and ones, and check one another's work.

My favorite movie is one hundred twenty-six minutes long. That's the same as 126 or 100 + 20 + 6.

Read and Write Three-Digit Numbers

Name: _____

Prerequisite: Write Three-Digit Numbers as Hundreds, Tens, and Ones

Study the example showing how to write hundreds, tens, and ones. Then solve Problems 1–5.

Example

How many hundreds, tens, and ones are in 214?

Use a model.

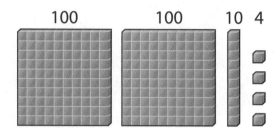

100   100   10   4

Write in a chart.

Hundreds	Tens	Ones
2	1	4

2 hundreds + 1 ten + 4 ones

---

1 How many hundreds, tens, and ones are in 332?

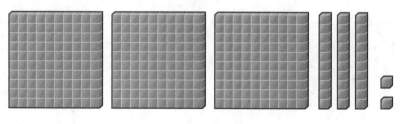

_____ hundreds + _____ tens + _____ ones

2 Complete the chart to show 7 hundreds + 5 tens + 8 ones.

Hundreds	Tens	Ones

Solve.

3 This model shows 243 in tens. How many tens are in 243? How many ones are left over?

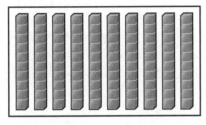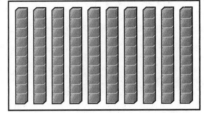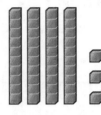

243 = _____ tens and _____ ones

4 Show 492 in two different ways.

Hundreds	Tens	Ones

5 Greg did this problem. What did he do wrong? Explain.

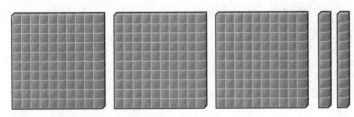

3 hundreds + 2 tens = 32

_____

_____

_____

_____

Name: _____

Find the Value of Three-Digit Numbers

Study the example about showing three-digit numbers in different ways. Then solve Problems 1–6.

Example

In a game, Jan pays money to the bank. She pays 2 hundreds bills, 4 tens bills, and 5 ones bills. What is the total value of the bills Jan pays?

Write a number sentence.

$200 + 40 + 5 = 245$ dollars

Make a quick drawing.

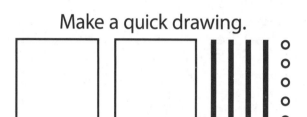

Use a chart.

Hundreds	Tens	Ones
2	4	5

Bob plays a board game that uses play money. He wins 3 hundreds bills, 7 tens bills, and 7 ones bills.

1　How many hundreds, tens, and ones are there?

_____ hundreds _____ tens _____ ones

2　Write a number sentence to find the total value of the bills.

_____ + _____ + _____ = _____

3　What is the total value of the bills Bob wins?

_____ dollars

Vocabulary

digit a symbol used to write numbers. The digits are: 0, 1, 2, 3, 4, 5, 6, 7, 8, 9.

value how much something is worth.

Solve.

4 Ali plays a board game that uses play money. He wins 8 hundreds bills and 6 ones bills. What is the total value of the bills Ali wins? Fill in the chart, then write the answer.

Hundreds	Tens	Ones

Show your work.

Answer: _____

5 Audra has 533 comic books. Write or draw to show this number in a different way.

6 What is another way to show each number? Draw lines to connect each number to another way to write the number.

784	874	748
800 + 70 + 4	700 + 80 + 4	700 + 40 + 8

Name: _____

Read and Write Three-Digit Numbers

Solve the problems.

1 Which number is the same as 800 + 30?
Circle the correct answer.

A 803   **C** 830

B 83   **D** 308

Can you use a chart to help you?

2 Bev wrote these clues about her secret number.

• The number has 5 hundreds.

• The tens digit is 1 less than 9.

• The number has more ones than tens.

What is the number? Circle the correct answer.

A 589   **C** 959

B 598   **D** 590

In a three-digit number, where is the tens digit?

3 What is true about the number 720?
Circle all the correct answers.

A It equals 72 tens.

B It is 700 + 2.

C It has 7 hundreds and 20 ones.

D It is 700 + 20.

How many hundreds, tens, and ones are in 720?

Solve.

4 Here are clues about a secret number. What is the number?

- The hundreds digit has a value of 300.
- The tens digit is 1 less than 2.
- The ones digit is the same as the hundreds digit.

Show your work.

Can you write a number sentence to help you?

Answer: _____

5 What is another way to show 4 hundreds and 3 tens? Circle the correct answer.

How can you show 3 tens?

A 43   **C** 403

B 400 + 3   **D** 400 + 30

Zack chose **C**. This is wrong. How did Zack get his answer?

_____

_____

_____

Dear Family,

This week your child is learning how to compare three-digit numbers.

Your child might see a problem like this: Ms. Perez drove 234 miles. Mr. Lee drove 213 miles. Who drove more miles?

You can model both numbers using quick drawings.

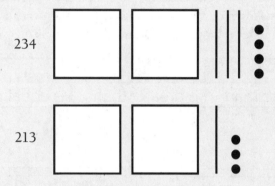

You can see that both models show 2 hundreds with 2 squares. But the top model shows 3 tens (with 3 lines) and the bottom model shows only 1 ten. So, the top model shows more. You don't have to compare ones, because there are already more tens in the top model.

The model shows that 234 is greater than 213, which we write as 234 > 213. So, we know that Ms. Perez drove more miles.

Invite your child to share what he or she knows about comparing three-digit numbers by doing the following activity together.

Comparing Three-Digit Numbers Activity

Materials: food or other items with weights listed on their labels (three-digit numbers), such as cans of fruit, boxes of dry cereal, and boxes of crackers; paper and pencil

- With your child, choose two items that seem to be about the same size (or use the sample boxes below). Write down the number of ounces or grams inside, as shown on the label for each item.

- Ask your child to compare the number of grams or the number of ounces. Encourage your child to use comparison words and symbols as shown in the table below. (Example: Cracker Brand A's weight is greater than Cracker Brand B's. 408 > 397)

<	>	=
is less than	is greater than	is equal to

Cracker Brand A

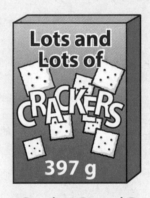

Cracker Brand B

Compare Three-Digit Numbers

Name: _____

Study the example showing how to compare two-digit numbers. Then solve Problems 1–7.

Example

Write <, >, or = in the blank.

<	>	=
is less than	is greater than	is equal to

76 $\leq$ 85 ← Compare the tens.
7 tens is less than 8 tens.

34 $\geq$ 32 ← The tens are the same. So compare the ones. 4 ones is greater than 2 ones.

Mike has 64 stickers. Nora has 38 stickers.

1 How many tens and ones are in each number?

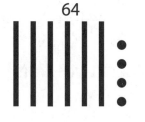
64

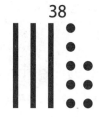
38

_____ tens _____ ones   _____ tens _____ ones

2 Compare the tens.

_____ tens is greater than _____ tens.

3 Compare the numbers. Write <, >, or = in the blank.

64 _____ 38

Solve.

4 Write $<$, $>$, or $=$ in the blank.

45 _____ 41   26 _____ 26

92 _____ 35   54 _____ 57

5 Write 23 and 27 as tens and ones. Then write a number sentence to compare the two numbers.

23: _____ tens _____ ones

27: _____ tens _____ ones

_____

6 Write a number sentence to compare 96 and 93. Explain why the number sentence is true.

_____

_____

7 Use these digits: 9, 3, 4, 8. Write the greatest and smallest two-digit numbers that you can. Tell how you got your answer.

_____

_____

_____

_____

Name: _____

Compare Three-Digit Numbers

Study the example showing how to compare three-digit numbers. Then solve Problems 1–8.

Example

Compare 217 and 234.

217 = 2 hundreds + 1 ten + 7 ones

234 = 2 hundreds + 3 tens + 4 ones

The hundreds are the same.
Compare the tens.

1 ten is less than 3 tens.

217 < 234

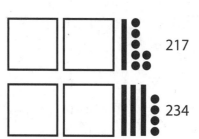

Cam has 482 marbles. Joe has 439 marbles.

1 How many hundreds, tens, and ones are in each number?

482 = _____ hundreds _____ tens _____ ones

439 = _____ hundreds _____ tens _____ ones

2 The hundreds are the same. Compare the tens.

_____ tens is greater than _____ tens.

3 Complete the number sentence.

_____ > _____

4 Use the same numbers as Problem 3. Write a different number sentence.

_____

Solve.

Vince and Rina guess how many paper clips are in a box. Vince guesses 195, and Rina guesses 172.

5 How many hundreds, tens, and ones are in each number?

195 = _____ hundred _____ tens _____ ones

172 = _____ hundred _____ tens _____ ones

6 Complete the number sentence.

_____ < _____

Mel has 938 stamps in her stamp collection. Yuri has 926 stamps in his stamp collection.

7 Write two different number sentences to compare 938 and 926.

_____ < _____ and _____ > _____

8 Explain why your number sentences in Problem 7 are true.

_____

_____

_____

Name: _____

Compare Three-Digit Numbers

Study the example showing how to compare three-digit numbers. Then solve Problems 1–8.

Example

Compare 528 and 523.

Hundreds	Tens	Ones
5	2	8
5	2	3

The hundreds are the same.
The tens are the same.
Compare the ones.

8 ones is greater than 3 ones.

528 > 523 and 523 < 528

Ned and Vera are playing a game. Ned has 142 points, and Vera has 147 points.

1 Write the numbers in the chart.

Hundreds	Tens	Ones

2 Complete the number sentence to compare 142 and 147.

_____ > _____

3 Which place did you have to look at to compare 142 and 147? Why?

_____

_____

Solve.

4 Complete two different number sentences to compare 824 and 829.

_____ > _____ and _____ < _____

5 Complete two different number sentences to compare 353 and 351.

_____ > _____ and _____ < _____

6 Complete two different number sentences to compare 675 and 629.

_____ > _____ and _____ < _____

7 Write >, <, or = in each blank.

a. 465 _____ 467

b. 392 _____ 356

c. 885 _____ 882

d. 214 _____ 312

e. 691 _____ 691

f. 484 _____ 394

8 Below are Han's scores in a game. Which game has the greatest score? Which game has the lowest score? Tell how you know.

Game 1: 328
Game 2: 289
Game 3: 325

_____

_____

_____

Name: _____

Compare Three-Digit Numbers

Solve the problems.

1 In one week, Glen read for 317 minutes. Fran read for 372 minutes. Who read for more minutes? Tell how you know.

Show your work.

Are you looking for the smaller or greater number?

Answer: _____

2 Choose *True* or *False* for each number sentence.

Which place value should you compare first?

a. $131 < 119$	True	False
b. $605 = 650$	True	False
c. $454 > 451$	True	False
d. $709 < 722$	True	False

3 Marcy had 237 stickers. Then she gave some stickers away. How many stickers could she have now? Circle all the correct answers.

Does Marcy have more than or less than 237 stickers now?

A 239	**C** 229
B 198	**D** 323

Solve.

4 Which number sentence is true? Circle the correct answer.

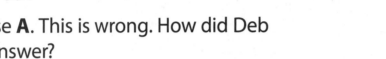

You can rewrite the numbers that are shown as tens and ones.

A 420 < 4 hundreds 3 ones

B 370 > 407

C 6 hundreds 4 tens < 640

D 919 < 991

Deb chose **A**. This is wrong. How did Deb get her answer?

_____

_____

5 Use the digits 5, 2, and 9 to make the smallest three-digit number that you can. Explain how you got your answer.

I think I will choose the digit for the hundreds place first.

_____

_____

_____

6 Use the digit cards from Problem 5 to make the greatest three-digit number that you can. Write the number below.

Which is the greatest digit?

_____

Dear Family,

This week your child is learning different strategies to add three-digit numbers.

Here are some ways he or she might find the sum 237 + 311.

Add hundreds, tens, and ones.

$$237 \longrightarrow 200 + 30 + 7$$
$$\underline{+\ 311} \longrightarrow \underline{300 + 10 + 1}$$
$$ 500 + 40 + 8$$

Break numbers into hundreds, tens, and ones.

$$237 \longrightarrow 2 \text{ hundreds} + 3 \text{ tens} + 7 \text{ ones}$$
$$\underline{+\ 311} \longrightarrow \underline{3 \text{ hundreds} + 1 \text{ ten } + 1 \text{ one}}$$
$$ 5 \text{ hundreds} + 4 \text{ tens} + 8 \text{ ones}$$

Add ones, then tens, then hundreds.

$$237$$
$$\underline{+\ 311}$$
$$8 \longleftarrow \quad 7 + 1$$
$$40 \longleftarrow \quad 30 + 10$$
$$\underline{+\ 500} \longleftarrow \ 200 + 300$$
$$548$$

> 500 + 40 + 8,
> 5 hundreds + 4 tens + 8 ones, and
> 548 are all the same.
> 237 + 311 = 548

Invite your child to share what he or she knows about adding three-digit numbers by doing the following activity together.

Adding Three-Digit Numbers Activity

Do this activity with your child to provide practice in adding three-digit numbers, as well as some practice in estimating sums.

- Ask your child to come up with a three-digit number less than 500. This will be the "special" number. (Example: Your child picks 385.)

- Have your child ask a family member for a three-digit number less than 500. (Example: The family member picks 209.)

- Ask your child if he or she thinks the sum of that number and the "special" number will be greater than or less than 500. (Example: Your child says it will be greater than 500.)

- Have your child add the two numbers to check his or her answer. (Example: $385 + 209 = 594$; your child was correct.)

- Repeat the process with other family members or the same person.

Do you think 453 + 100 will be more or less than 500?

Add Three-Digit Numbers

Name: _____

Study the example showing how to add two-digit numbers. Then solve Problems 1–7.

Example

Find $27 + 16$.

You can add tens and add ones.

$27 = 20 + 7$
$16 = 10 + 6$
$\overline{ 30 + 13 = 43}$

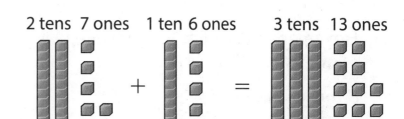

2 tens 7 ones   1 ten 6 ones   3 tens 13 ones

There are 48 red grapes and 24 green grapes in a salad.

1 Write the tens and ones.

$48 = $ _____ $+$ _____

$24 = $ _____ $+$ _____

2 Add the tens. Then add the ones.

_____ $+$ _____ $= 60$

_____ $+$ _____ $= 12$

3 Show how to find how many grapes there are in all.

_____

_____

Solve.

Luke played piano for 58 minutes yesterday. He played piano for 27 minutes today.

4 Write the tens and ones.

58 = _____ + _____

27 = _____ + _____

5 How many total minutes did Luke play piano?

Show your work.

Answer: _____ minutes

Ms. Patel has 29 blue pens, 17 red pens, and 35 red crayons.

6 How many red pens and red crayons does Ms. Patel have?

Show your work.

Answer: _____

7 How many blue pens and red pens does Ms. Patel have?

Show your work.

Answer: _____

Name: _____

Add Hundreds, Tens, and Ones

Study the example showing two ways to add three-digit numbers. Then solve Problems 1–7.

Example

Solve $227 + 135$.

You can make a quick drawing. ⟶

You can break apart the addends.

$$
\begin{array}{r}
227 \longrightarrow 200 + 20 + 7 \\
+\ 135 \longrightarrow 100 + 30 + 5 \\
\hline
300 + 50 + 12
\end{array}
$$

$227 + 135 = 362$

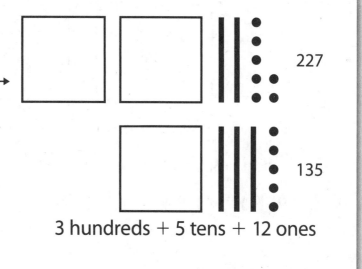

227

135

3 hundreds + 5 tens + 12 ones

There are 416 oak trees and 238 pine trees in the park.

1 Fill in the boxes to help you find the total.

$$
\begin{array}{r}
416 \longrightarrow 400 + 10 + 6 \\
+\ 238 \longrightarrow 200 + 30 + 8 \\
\hline
\boxed{} + \boxed{} + 14
\end{array}
$$

2 14 ones = _____ ten + _____ ones

3 How many trees are there altogether?

_____ trees

Solve.

Paul has 547 beads. Amy has 219 beads.

4 Fill in the boxes.

$$547 \rightarrow 500 + 40 + 7$$
$$+ 219 \rightarrow \boxed{} + \boxed{} + \boxed{}$$
$$\boxed{} + \boxed{} + \boxed{}$$

5 Add hundreds, tens, and ones to solve.
Show your work.

_____ beads

A zoo has 146 birds and 628 bugs. It also has 258 snakes and 338 fish.

6 How many birds and bugs are there?
Show your work.

$$\begin{array}{r} 146 \\ + 628 \\ \hline \end{array}$$

Answer: _____

7 How many snakes and fish are there?
Show your work.

$258 + 338$

Answer: _____

Name: _____

Add Three-Digit Numbers

Study the example showing how to add hundreds, tens, and ones. Then solve Problems 1–5.

Example

Solve 346 + 487.

You can add hundreds,
then tens, then ones.

$$
\begin{array}{r}
346 \\
+\ 487 \\
\hline
\end{array}
$$

700 → 300 + 400
120 → 40 + 80
13 → 6 + 7

700 + 120 + 13 = 833

You can add ones, then tens,
then hundreds.

$$
\begin{array}{r}
346 \\
+\ 487 \\
\hline
\end{array}
$$

13 → 6 + 7
120 → 40 + 80
700 → 300 + 400

13 + 120 + 700 = 833

Mina's class collects 368 cans to recycle.
Willa's class collects 254 cans.

1 Fill in the boxes to show how you can add
hundreds, then tens, then ones.

$$
\begin{array}{r}
368 \\
+\ 254 \\
\hline
\end{array}
$$

☐

110

☐

2 How many cans do the classes
collect altogether?

_____ + 110 + _____ = _____

Solve.

3 Show how to find 579 + 358.

4 Show how you can add 157 and 296.

5 Use the numbers in the box. Find the greatest sum that you can. Then find the smallest sum. Tell how you got your answer.

| 268 | 275 | 242 | 259 |

_____

_____

_____

Name: _____

Add Three-Digit Numbers

Solve the problems.

1 Charlie has 378 play coins. Ting has 147. How many coins do Charlie and Ting have in all?

Show your work.

Will you add hundreds or ones first?

Answer: _____

2 A flower store sells 285 roses in the morning and 260 roses in the afternoon. Which addition problem shows how many roses the store sells in all? Circle the correct answer.

How many hundreds, tens, and ones does each number have?

A 200 + 140 + 50

B 200 + 140 + 5

C 400 + 140 + 5

D 400 + 140 + 50

Lance chose **B**. This is wrong. How did Lance get his answer?

_____

_____

Solve.

3 Find 426 + 315. Write the missing numbers on the open number line below.

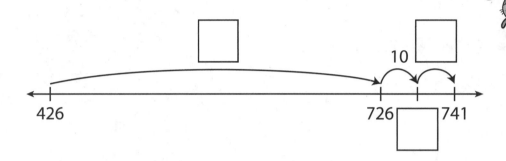

What number do you add to 426 to get to 726?

4 Macy needs to double the number 439. What addition problem can she use? Circle all the correct answers.

A 18 + 60 + 800

B 400 + 60 + 18

C 800 + 60 + 10 + 8

D 800 + 60 + 90

What are the two numbers in the addition problem?

5 Elsa writes 500 + 70 + 6. What two-digit numbers could she be adding? Circle the correct answer.

A 371 + 275   **C** 403 + 273

B 145 + 421   **D** 252 + 324

Which two digits should I add to get 500?

Dear Family,

This week your child is learning to subtract three-digit numbers using place value.

For example, your child might be asked to find $403 - 279$.

The numbers can be organized by place value in a chart.

$403 = 4$ hundreds $+ 0$ tens $+ 3$ ones
$279 = 2$ hundreds $+ 7$ tens $+ 9$ ones

There are not enough ones to subtract $403 - 279$.

100s	10s	1s
4	0	3
2	7	9

$4 > 2 \quad 0 < 7 \quad \boxed{3 < 9}$

Regroup a hundred and a ten in 403 to get 10 more ones.
4 hundreds $+ 0$ tens $+ 3$ ones
$\quad = 3$ hundreds $+ 10$ tens $+ 3$ ones
$\quad = 3$ hundreds $+ 9$ tens $+ 13$ ones

100s	10s	1s
4	0	3
3	10	3
3	9	13

Now, subtract 279.

$\begin{array}{r} 3 \text{ hundreds} + 9 \text{ tens} + 13 \text{ ones} \\ - \ 2 \text{ hundreds} + 7 \text{ tens} + \ 9 \text{ ones} \\ \hline 1 \text{ hundred} \ + 2 \text{ tens} + \ 4 \text{ ones} \end{array}$

100s	10s	1s
3	9	13
2	7	9
1	2	4

$403 - 279 = 124$

Invite your child to share what he or she knows about subtracting three-digit numbers by doing the following activity together.

Subtracting Three-Digit Numbers Activity

Materials: catalogs, ads, online retailers

Do this activity with your child to practice subtraction. This activity will also help him or her see how subtraction is used in the real world.

- Talk with your child about something the family would like to buy. Think about items that cost between $100 and $1,000.

- Look through catalogs, ads, or web sites to find prices for the item, or use the sample catalog pages below. Only use the whole number parts of prices. (Example: If a TV costs $979.99, have your child use the price $979.)

- Ask your child at which store the item is the least expensive. Help your child use subtraction to compare prices and find out how much less the item costs at one store compared to another.

Andy's Appliances

Washing machine... $699
Dryer.............. $590
Refrigerator........ $548
Oven $475
Microwave......... $178

Main Street Home Store

Washing machine... $752
Dryer.............. $564
Refrigerator........ $499
Oven $482
Microwave......... $205

Subtract Three-Digit Numbers

Name: _____

Study the example showing one way to subtract two-digit numbers. Then solve Problems 1–6.

Example

Find 64 − 27.

64 − 27 = ? is the same as 27 + ? = 64.
Add up.

27 + 30 = 57

57 + 3 = 60

60 + 4 = 64

30 + 3 + 4 = 37

64 − 27 = 37

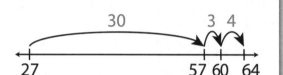

Ed has 76 red and yellow tulips. There are 28 red tulips. How many tulips are yellow?

1 Find 76 − 28 by adding up. Fill in the blanks on the number line.

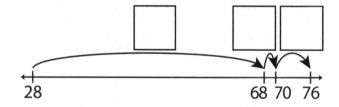

2 Add to find the number of yellow tulips. Fill in the blanks.

_____ + _____ + _____ = _____

Solve.

There were 35 birds in a tree. Then 17 birds flew away. How many birds are in the tree now?

3 Regroup a ten first. Fill in the blank.

35 = 2 tens and _____ ones

4. Find 35 − 17. Subtract tens and ones.

Show your work.

Answer: _____ birds left

Hector and Rose each have 93 baseball cards. Hector gives 54 cards to his brother. Rose gives 48 cards to her friend.

5 How many baseball cards does Hector have now? Find 93 − 54.

Show your work.

Answer: _____

6 How many baseball cards does Rose have now? Find 93 − 48.

Show your work.

Answer: _____

Subtract Hundreds, Tens, and Ones

Study the example showing one way to subtract three-digit numbers. Then solve Problems 1–6.

Example

Find $874 - 235$. Look at the ones: 4 ones $<$ 5 ones. Regroup a ten in 874 as 10 ones.

$874 = 800 + 70 + 4$, or $800 + 60 + 14$

$$\begin{array}{r} 800 + 60 + 14 \\ -\ 200 + 30 + \ \ 5 \\ \hline 600 + 30 + \ \ 9 = 639 \end{array}$$

$874 - 235 = 639$

There are 546 students at Lincoln School. On Mondays, 327 students have art class. The rest have music class.

1 Find $546 - 327$. First regroup a ten. Write the new ones. Then subtract.

$$\begin{array}{r} 500 + \ 30 \ + \boxed{} \\ -\ 300 + \ 20 \ + \ \ 7 \\ \hline \boxed{} + \boxed{} + \boxed{} \end{array}$$

2 How many students have music class?

_____

3 You can subtract hundreds, tens, and ones. Fill in the blanks.

$546 - 300 =$ _____

$246 - 20 =$ _____

$226 - 7 =$ _____

Solve.

4 472 people saw the school play. On Saturday, 248 people saw the play. The rest saw it on Sunday. How many people saw the play on Sunday?

Show your work.

Answer: _____

5 Children made 220 paintings for the city art show. Girls made 117 paintings. How many paintings did boys make?

Show your work.

Answer: _____

6 Blake has 583 stickers. Sasha has 324 fewer stickers than Blake. How many stickers do they have in all?

Show your work.

Answer: _____

Name: _____

Regroup to Subtract Three-Digit Numbers

Study the example showing how to regroup to subtract three-digit numbers. Then solve Problems 1–7.

Example

Find $512 - 367$.

Compare the digits in each place.

5 hundreds	+	1 ten	+	2 ones
3 hundreds	+	6 tens	+	7 ones
$5 > 3$		$1 < 6$		$2 < 7$

Regroup 512 two times.

$500 + 10 + 2$
$= 400 + 100 + 10 + 2$
$= 400 + 100 + 12$

100s	10s	1s
4	10	12
− 3	6	7
1	4	5

$512 - 367 = 145$

Jodi's book has 423 pages. She has read 275 pages. Her father asks her how many pages she has left.

1 Compare the digits in each place. Write $<$ or $>$ in each box.

4 hundreds	+	2 tens	+	3 ones
2 hundreds	+	7 tens	+	5 ones

4 ☐ 2   2 ☐ 7   3 ☐ 5

2 Show how to regroup. Fill in the blanks.

$400 + 20 + 3$
$= 300 + \_\_\_\_\_ + 10 + 10 + \_\_\_\_\_$
$= 300 + 110 + \_\_\_\_\_$

100s	10s	1s
3	11	☐
− 2	7	5
☐	☐	☐

3 Fill in the chart to show the regrouping. Then subtract each place.

Solve.

4 Fill in the blanks to show how you can add up to find 215 − 157.

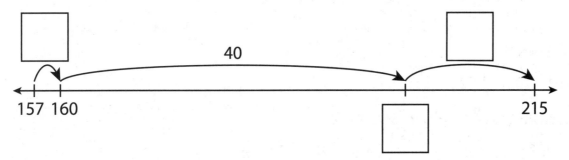

40

157 160   215

5 How do you use the open number line in Problem 4 to find 215 − 157?

_____

6 Ken has 442 paper clips. There are 379 small paper clips. The rest are large. How many large paper clips are there?

Show your work.

Answer: _____

7 Tim solved a subtraction problem. Write a number sentence to show the problem and answer. Tell how you got your answer.

Tim's Answer:
863 + 7 = 870
870 + 30 = 900
900 + 50 = 950

_____

_____

_____

Name: _____

Subtract Three-Digit Numbers

Solve the problems.

1 Fill in the blanks to find 524 − 335.

100s	10s	1s
4	☐	14
− 3	3	5
☐	☐	☐

How many times do you need to regroup?

2 Sally has 237 marbles. Gina has 184 marbles. How many more marbles does Sally have? Circle the correct answer.

A 157   **C** 87

B 153   **D** 53

How could you add up to find the answer?

3 For each subtraction problem, tell if you need to regroup tens to get more ones. Then tell if you need to regroup hundreds. Circle *Yes* or *No* for Tens and Hundreds for each problem.

I can compare ones digits to see if I need to regroup tens.

	Tens	**Hundreds**
a. 643 − 225	Yes No	Yes No
b. 812 − 511	Yes No	Yes No
c. 574 − 396	Yes No	Yes No
d. 709 − 488	Yes No	Yes No

Solve.

4 There are 951 people in a parade. There are 728 people marching. The rest ride on floats. How many people ride on floats?

Show your work.

You can add up or subtract hundreds, tens, and ones.

Answer: _____

5 Mr. Grant had 357 plums for sale. He sold some of them. Now he has 219 plums. How many plums did Mr. Grant sell? Circle the correct answer.

How many hundreds, tens, and ones are in each number?

A 38   **C** 148

B 147   **D** 138

Matt chose **C**. This is wrong. How did Matt get his answer?

_____

_____

_____

Dear Family,

This week your child is learning different ways to add three or more two-digit numbers.

Here are some ways he or she might add 18 + 34 + 22 + 26.

- One way is to break each number into tens and ones and then add pairs of numbers.

Tens	Ones
1 > 4	8 > 12
3	4
2 > 4	2 > 8
2	6

$$4 \text{ tens} + 4 \text{ tens} + 12 \text{ ones} + 8 \text{ ones}$$
$$8 \text{ tens} + 20 \text{ ones}$$
$$80 + 20 = 100$$

So, 18 + 34 + 22 + 26 = 100.

- Another way is to add two numbers at a time. If you can find pairs of numbers with ones digits that make a 10, add those first.

$$18 + 34 + 22 + 26$$
$$40 + 60 = 100$$

> 8 + 2 = 10, so add 18 + 22.
> 4 + 6 = 10, so add 34 + 26.

So, 18 + 34 + 22 + 26 = 100.

Invite your child to share what he or she knows about adding three or more two-digit numbers by doing the following activity together.

NEXT

Adding Two-Digit Numbers Activity

- Work with your child to solve the following problem.

  A school is holding a math team competition. Each team has four students. The team score is the sum of the four students' scores. Which team won the competition?

Tigers
35
68
42
55

Lions
67
88
41
39

Bears
56
62
44
63

Hawks
35
90
28
60

- Ask your child to add the four scores on each team.
  (Tigers: 200; Lions: 235; Bears: 225; Hawks: 213)

- Work with your child to compare the totals to find the winner.

- Ask your child to make up a new team. Ask your child what scores he or she could give each student on the new team in order to win the competition.

Add Several Two-Digit Numbers

Name: _____

Prerequisite: Add Two-Digit Numbers

Study the example showing how to go to the next ten to add two-digit numbers. Then solve Problems 1–7.

Example

Add 48 + 37.

You can go to the next ten first.

48 + 2 = 50

Then add the tens.

50 + 30 = 80

Then add the rest of the ones.

80 + 5 = 85   48 + 37 = 85

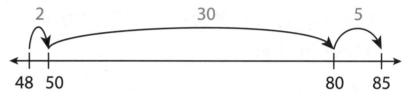

Grace walked for 26 minutes. Later, she walked for 48 minutes more. For how many minutes did Grace walk in all?

1 How many ones do you add to go to the next ten? Fill in the blank on the number line.

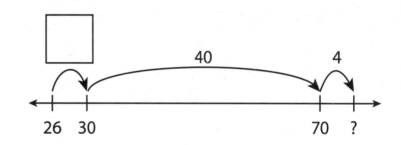

2 Add the tens.   30 + 40 = _____

3 Add the rest of the ones.   70 + 4 = _____

4 For how many minutes did Grace walk?   _____ minutes

Solve.

5 Felix had 38 bookmarks. Then he made 25 more. How many bookmarks does Felix have now? Fill in the boxes. Then solve the problem.

Felix has _____ bookmarks now.

$$38 = 30 + \boxed{}$$

$$25 = \boxed{} + \boxed{}$$

$$\boxed{} + \boxed{}$$

6 There are 18 students in Ms. Tan's class. There are 23 students in Mr. Leed's class. How many students are in both classes?

Show your work.

Answer: _____

7 Frank uses 57 blocks to build a tower. Then he uses 35 more blocks to make it taller. How many blocks does Frank use in all?

Show your work.

Answer: _____

Add Four Two-Digit Numbers

Study the example showing different ways to add four two-digit numbers. Then solve Problems 1–7.

Example

Add 27, 32, 43, and 65.

You can look for numbers with ones that make a ten.

Add those numbers first.

$$7 + 3 = 10$$

27 + 32 + 43 + 65

70 + 97 = 167

You can break each number into tens and ones. Then add.

$$
\begin{array}{r}
20 + 7 \\
30 + 2 \\
40 + 3 \\
60 + 5 \\
\hline
150 + 17 = 167
\end{array}
$$

$$27 + 32 + 43 + 65 = 167$$

Mr. Dell ran four times last week. He ran for 25, 27, 28, and 32 minutes.

1 Which two numbers have ones that make a ten? Add those first.

$$28 + \rule{2cm}{0.4pt} = 60$$

2 Add the other two numbers.

$$25 + 27 = \rule{2cm}{0.4pt}$$

3 Show how to find the total minutes Mr. Dell ran.

_____

_____

Solve.

There are 47 apples and 49 pears for sale at the farm stand. There are also 53 peaches and 62 plums.

4 Break each number into tens and ones. Write your answers in the box.

47 = _____ + _____

49 = _____ + _____

53 = _____ + _____

62 = _____ + _____

5 How many pieces of fruit are there in all?

Show your work.

6 Abby plays four games of cards. She gets 29, 34, 36, and 52 points. What is the total number of points Abby gets?

Show your work.

Answer: _____

7 Dom has 21 red blocks and 24 blue blocks. He has 29 green blocks and 35 pink blocks. How many blocks does Dom have?

Show your work.

Answer: _____

Name: _____

Add Several Two-Digit Numbers

Solve the problems.

1 People from Rico's school help clean up the park. The chart shows how many people do each job. How many people clean up the park?

Rake Leaves	Plant Flowers	Paint Benches
42	49	18

Which two numbers will you add first?

Show your work.

Answer: _____

2 Sid adds these numbers.

$51 + 18 + 19 + 38$

How can Sid add these numbers? Circle all the correct answers.

A $70 + 56$　　　**C** $90 + 57$

B $80 + 67$　　　**D** $100 + 26$

Remember, you can add tens and then ones. Or you can make a ten first.

Solve.

3 Pete is jumping rope. He does 38, 50, 22, and 29 jumps. How many jumps does he do in all? Circle the correct answer.

A 94   **C** 139

B 114   **D** 179

Jess chose **A**. This is wrong. How did Jess get her answer?

_____

_____

4 Complete each number sentence using a number from the green box.

a. 26 + ☐ = 100

b. ☐ + 61 = 100

c. 52 + ☐ = 100

| 39 |
| 48 |
| 74 |

5 Meg's garden has 31 daisies, 16 roses, 25 tulips, and 34 sunflowers. How many flowers are in Meg's garden?

Show your work.

Answer: _____

Unit 2 Game

3-Digit Number Comparing

What you need: Recording Sheet, 6 sets of Digit Cards (0–9)

Directions

- Mix the Digit Cards. Each player gets 5 cards. Choose one player to be Player A and one to be Player B.

- In each round, each player uses 3 of his or her cards to make a 3-digit number.

- The player with the greater number wins all 6 cards. If the numbers are equal, each player uses at least one different card to make a new number.

- After each round, write the two numbers on the Recording Sheet, then use them to complete the number sentence.

- Players take 3 new Digit Cards to fill their hands. Play 8 rounds. The player who wins the most cards wins the game.

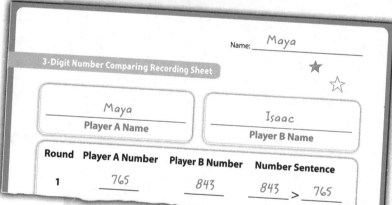

Round	Player A Number	Player B Number	Number Sentence
1	765	843	843 > 765

Name: Maya

3-Digit Number Comparing Recording Sheet

Maya — Player A Name

Isaac — Player B Name

I used 3, 4, and 8 to make 843. I win because 843 is greater than 765.

Name: _____

_____	_____
Player A Name	**Player B Name**

Round	Player A Number	Player B Number	Number Sentence
1	_____	_____	_____ > _____
2	_____	_____	_____ > _____
3	_____	_____	_____ > _____
4	_____	_____	_____ > _____
5	_____	_____	_____ > _____
6	_____	_____	_____ > _____
7	_____	_____	_____ > _____
8	_____	_____	_____ > _____

I played with _____.

He/She won [ ] **cards.**

I won [ ] **cards.**

✂

0	1	2	3	4
5	6	7	8	9
0	1	2	3	4
5	6	7	8	9

0	1	2	3	4
5	6	7	8	9
0	1	2	3	4
5	6	7	8	9

✄

0	1	2	3	4
5	6	7	8	9
0	1	2	3	4
5	6	7	8	9

Unit 2 Practice

Name: _____

Number and Operations in Base Ten

In this unit you learned to:	Lesson
add two-digit numbers.	7
add tens and add ones.	7
subtract two-digit numbers.	8
regroup a ten.	8
solve a one-step word problem by adding or subtracting two-digit numbers.	9
read and write three-digit numbers.	10, 11
compare three-digit numbers.	12
add three-digit numbers.	13
subtract three-digit numbers.	14
add more than two two-digit numbers.	15

Use these skills to solve Problems 1–6.

1 Complete the table to show 472 in different ways.

Hundreds	Tens	Ones
	7	2
2	6	
0		2

2 Scott adds the number of crayons in four boxes. What is the total? Circle the correct answer.

$$32 + 57 + 28 + 41$$

A 179   C 158

B 168   D 149

Solve.

3 How can you find $47 - 18$? Circle all the correct answers.

A $18 + 2 = 20$ and
$20 + 27 = 47; 2 + 27 = 29$

B $47 - 7 = 40$ and
$40 - 8 = 32$

C $47 - 10 = 37$ and
$37 - 8 = 29$

D
$$\begin{array}{r} 3 \text{ tens and } 17 \text{ ones} \\ - \ 1 \text{ ten and } 8 \text{ ones} \\ \hline 2 \text{ tens and } 9 \text{ ones} \end{array}$$

4 Tory has 308 stickers. Nina has 287 stickers. Compare the numbers. Write $>$ or $<$ in each blank.

308 _____ 287

287 _____ 308

5 Tory and Nina want to know how many stickers they have in all. How could they find $308 + 287$? Circle all the correct answers.

A $300 + 200 + 80 + 15$

B $308 + 200 + 80 + 7$

C $500 + 90 + 15$

D $500 + 80 + 8 + 7$

6 Ari had some shells. He gave away 26. Then he had 45 shells. How many shells did Ari have at the start?

Show your work.

Answer: _____

Name: _____

Answer the questions and show all your work on separate paper.

Last year, Jim's class picked up cans and bottles to recycle. They got 427 bottles and cans in all. Here are their goals for this year:

- Collect at least 100 more cans and bottles than last year.

- Collect at least 200 bottles.

- Collect at least 200 cans.

Make a plan for reaching the goals. Give the number of bottles and cans the class needs to collect. Tell why your numbers work.

Use the tools on the back of this page.

- Make a tape diagram to show the number of bottles and cans the class needs. Write the total.

- Write a number sentence to show that the total number of cans and bottles is at least 100 more than last year.

- Use the sentence starters to help you tell why your numbers work.

Reflect on Mathematical Practices

Reason Quantitatively How did you decide the numbers of bottles and cans to use for your answer?

©Curriculum Associates, LLC   Copying is not permitted.

Checklist

Did you . . .

☐ show all your work?

☐ make sure all your numbers fit the plan?

☐ show why your numbers work?

Word Bank Here are some words that you might use in your answer.

greater than	sum	total
enough	at least	compare
more	fewer	add
subtract	plus	minus

Models Here are some models that you can use to find the solution.

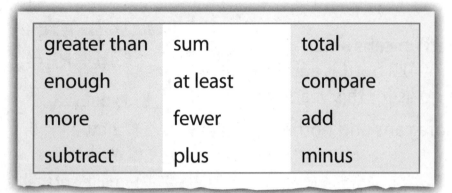

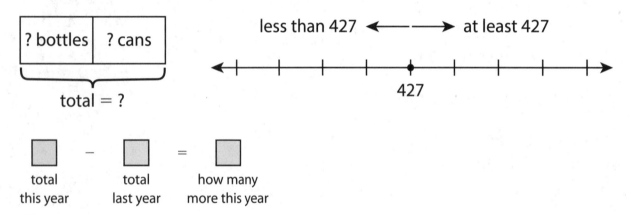

Sentence Starters Here are some sentence starters that can help you write an explanation.

_____ bottles and _____ cans

_____ greater than

The total number of bottles and cans _____

©Curriculum Associates, LLC   Copying is not permitted.

Unit 2 Vocabulary

Name: _____

My Examples

one-step problem

a word problem you can solve with one step

digit

a symbol used to write numbers. The digits are 0, 1, 2, 3, 4, 5, 6, 7, 8, and 9.

value

how much something is worth

My Words

_____

_____

_____

_____

My Words

_____

_____

_____

_____

_____

_____

_____

_____

_____

_____

_____

My Examples

Dear Family,

This week your child is exploring the importance of using standard units of measurement.

Your child will encounter measurements throughout their lives and it is important that he or she understands standard units of measurement.

You can describe the length of a pen, for example, using other objects. The pen to the right is 6 small paper clips long. However, it is important you don't use different-size objects when you measure, because you might not get the same measurement. If you used a mix of paper clip sizes, it wouldn't be clear what length 4 paper clips is.

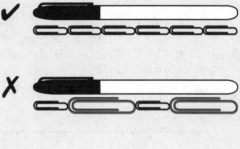

We use **standard units** to make sure that a measurement unit is always the same size, so that all measurements are consistent. Inches and centimeters are two examples of standard units.

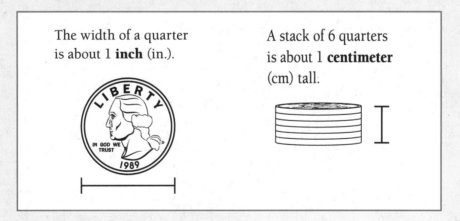

The width of a quarter is about 1 **inch** (in.).

A stack of 6 quarters is about 1 **centimeter** (cm) tall.

Invite your child to share what he or she knows about standard units of length by doing the following activity together.

NEXT

Lesson 16 Understand Length and Measurement Tools   **169**

Units of Measurement Activity

Remind your child that a ruler is a tool that measures using standard units.

- Cut out the ruler and 1-inch square tiles, or use an actual ruler and copy the tiles to a different sheet of paper and cut them out. Explain to your child that each square has a side length of 1 inch.

- Measure several objects by lining up the tiles side by side, then again using the ruler. (Measure all objects to the nearest inch. Explain to your child that means that if the length of an object falls between two inch measurements, pick the one that is closer to the length of the object.)

- Ask your child to explain why you get the same measurement using the tiles and using the ruler. Line up the tiles on top of the ruler to reinforce the fact that the ruler shows several inches side by side, just like the tiles.

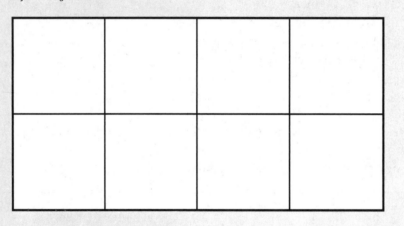

Do you think it's easier to use tiles or a ruler to measure an object? Why?

Name: _____

Prerequisite: How do you measure length correctly?

Study the example showing how to explain a measuring error. Then solve Problems 1–5.

Example

Lev says this string is
3 paper clips long.
Do you agree?
Why or why not?

No, the string needs to be placed at the edge of the first paper clip, not in the middle.

1 Juan used these paper clips to measure the pencil. What did he do wrong?

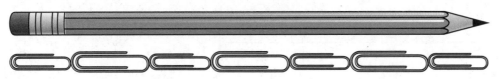

_____

_____

2 Callie says this ribbon is 4 paper clips long. Do you agree? Why or why not?

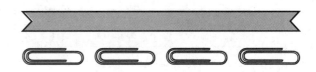

_____

_____

Solve.

3 Jill says this marker is 6 tiles long. Do you agree? Why or why not?

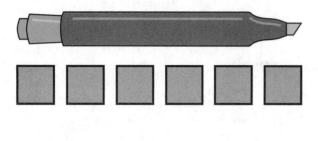

_____

_____

4 Sean says this crayon is 7 tiles long. Do you agree? Why or why not?

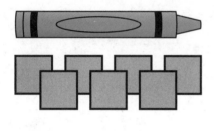

_____

_____

5 Circle the picture that shows the correct way to measure the piece of string.

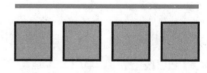

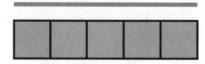

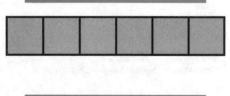

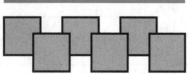

Name: _____

Measure with Tiles and Rulers

Study the example showing how to measure with tiles and rulers. Then solve Problems 1–7.

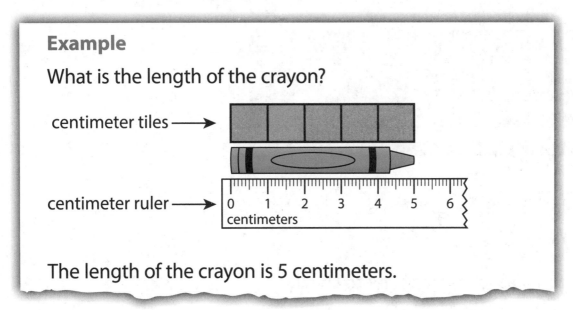

Example

What is the length of the crayon?

centimeter tiles ⟶

centimeter ruler ⟶

The length of the crayon is 5 centimeters.

1 Cai used 1-centimeter tiles to measure the length of a piece of string. How many tiles did he use? _____

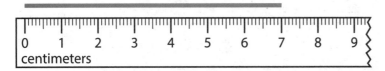

2 Each tile is 1 centimeter long. What is the length of the string? _____ centimeters

3 Cai used a centimeter ruler to check the length.

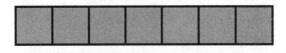

What is the length of the string?

_____

Lesson 16 Understand Length and Measurement Tools   **173**

Solve.

4 Emma used 1-inch tiles to measure the length of a piece of yarn. How many tiles did she use? _____

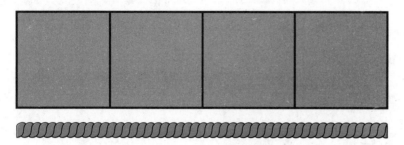

5 Each tile is 1 inch long. What is the length of the yarn? _____ inches

6 Then Emma used an inch ruler to check the length.

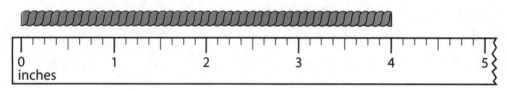

What is the length of the yarn? _____

7 Gus used 1-inch tiles and a ruler to measure the length of the pencil below.

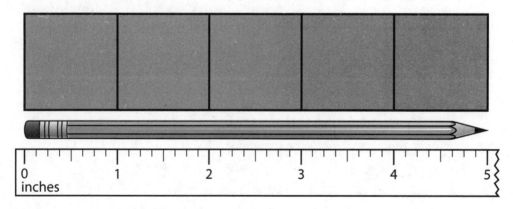

What is the length of the pencil? _____

Name: _____

Reason and Write

Look at the example. Underline a part that you think makes it a good answer.

Example

Bay used 1-centimeter tiles and a strip of paper to make the centimeter ruler below.

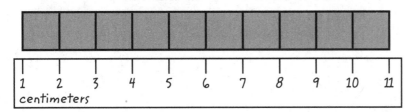

Bay wrote, My ruler is 11 centimeters long. What did Bay do right? What did she do wrong?

Use pictures, words, or numbers to explain.

Bay put the tiles above the paper strip. She lined up the tiles without any spaces between them and without the tiles on top of each other. She marked the beginning of the first tile on the paper strip. She also marked the end of each tile on the paper strip. All of that was correct.

Bay's only mistake was that she wrote 1 under the first mark. She should have written 0.

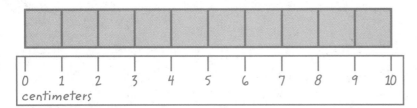

Then she would see that her ruler is 10 centimeters long.

Where does the example . . .

- explain what Bay did right?
- explain what Bay did wrong?
- use pictures, words, or numbers?

Solve the problem. Use what you learned from the example.

Jim used 1-inch tiles and a strip of paper to make the inch ruler below.

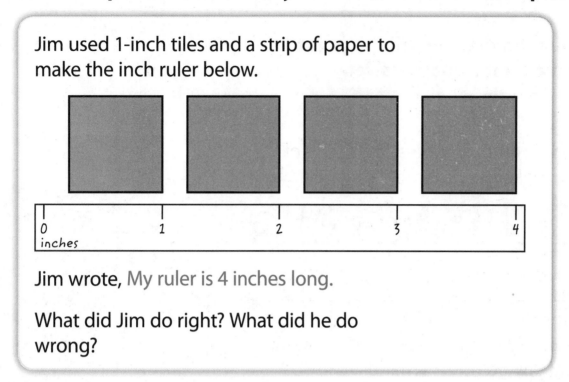

Jim wrote, My ruler is 4 inches long.

What did Jim do right? What did he do wrong?

Use pictures, words, or numbers to explain.

Did you . . .
- explain what Jim did right?
- explain what Jim did wrong?
- use pictures, words, or numbers?

Dear Family,

This week your child is learning how to use different measuring tools to measure the lengths of objects.

Your child will be introduced to the following measuring tools.

- A standard **ruler** usually shows 12 inches and is equal to 1 foot. It often also displays 30 centimeters.

- A **yardstick** shows 36 inches.

- A **meter stick** shows 100 centimeters.

- A **tape measure** shows inches and centimeters and is used to measure very long lengths.

How many inches long is this line? You can use a ruler to measure the length.

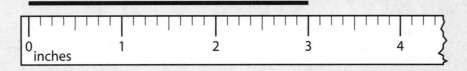

Line up the 0 with one end of the line. The 3 is at the other end of the line. So, the line is 3 inches long.

Different tools may be easier to use when measuring different objects. For example, it is easier to measure a crayon with a ruler than with a yardstick, but it's easier to measure the length of the couch with a yardstick than a ruler.

Invite your child to share what he or she knows about measuring length by doing the following activity together.

NEXT

Measuring Activity

Materials: measuring tool (ruler, yardstick, tape measure), household objects

Work with your child to practice measuring items around the house. Use whatever measuring tools you have available, or cut out the centimeter ruler to the right. Measure in inches or centimeters, depending on the tool you are using. Measure all objects to the nearest inch or centimeter. Explain to your child that means that if the length of an object falls between two inch or centimeter measurements, pick the one that is closer to the length of the object.

Ask your child to explain how he or she is measuring each item. Challenge your child to measure at least one object in each room of your home.

Remind your child to add the units of measurement when he or she fills in the table. For example, write the length of a pen as 6 inches, not 6.

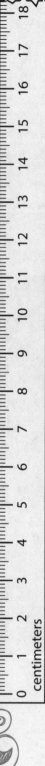

Object	Length

Measure Length

Prerequisite: Measure Using Tiles or a Ruler

Study the example showing how to measure length with inch tiles or a ruler. Then solve Problems 1–6.

Example

What is the length of the eraser?

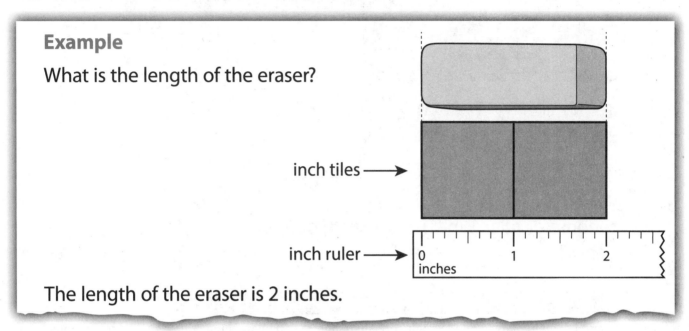

inch tiles ⟶

inch ruler ⟶

The length of the eraser is 2 inches.

1. Hugo measured this paintbrush using 1-inch tiles. How many tiles are there?

_____

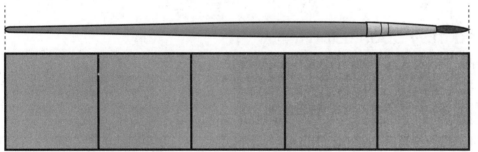

2. What is the length of the paintbrush?

_____ inches

3. Ron measured this marker using a 1-inch ruler. How long is the marker?

_____ inches

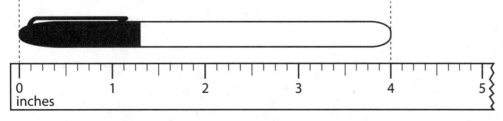

Solve.

4 Lucy measured this glue stick using
   1-centimeter tiles. How long is the glue
   stick?   _____ centimeters

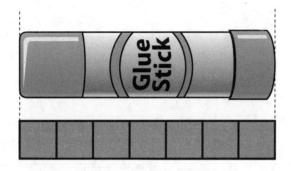

5 Ray measured this pencil using a
   centimeter ruler. What is the length of the
   pencil?   _____ centimeters

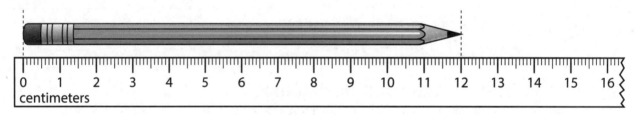

6 Eva measured this ribbon using a
   centimeter ruler. What did she do wrong?

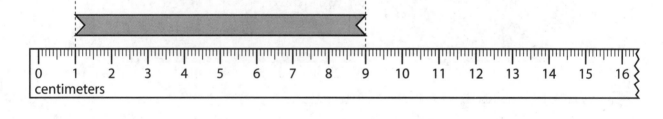

_____

_____

_____

Measure Length

Study the example showing how to measure length with centimeter tiles or a ruler. Then solve Problems 1–5.

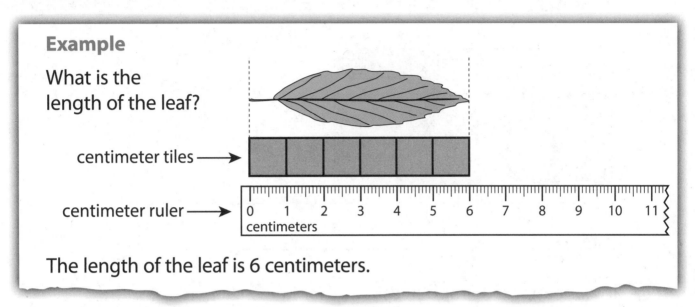

Example

What is the length of the leaf?

centimeter tiles ⟶

centimeter ruler ⟶

The length of the leaf is 6 centimeters.

---

1 Hal used 1-centimeter tiles to measure this craft stick. How long is the craft stick?

_____ centimeters

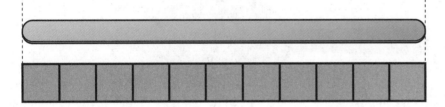

2 Beth measured this shell using a centimeter ruler. What is the length of the shell?

_____ centimeters

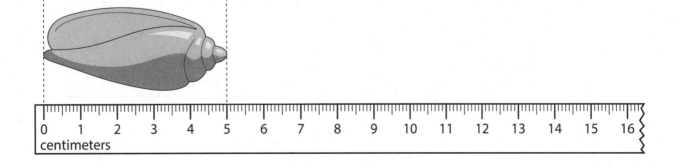

Solve.

3 Marty measured this marker using 1-inch tiles and an inch ruler. What is the length of the marker?

_____ inches

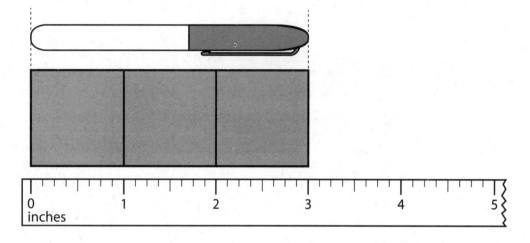

4 Toni measured this spoon using a centimeter ruler. What is the length of the spoon?

_____ centimeters

5 If you could measure something using a centimeter ruler or 1-centimeter tiles, which would you use? Why?

_____

_____

_____

Name: _____

More Ways to Measure Length

Study the example showing ways to measure an object. Then solve Problems 1–5.

Example

What is the length of the piece of yarn?

Use a ruler. The yarn is longer than a ruler. Mark where the ruler ends. Then move the ruler so that 0 is at your mark.

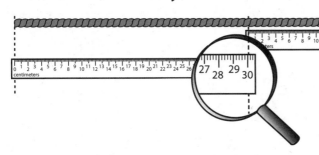

$30 \text{ cm} + 30 \text{ cm} = 60 \text{ cm}$

Or measure using a meter stick.

The piece of yarn is 60 centimeters long.

Nora wants to measure a piece of string. What is the length of the string?

The rulers and meter stick on this page are not life-sized.

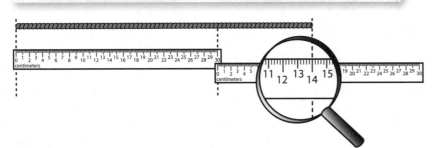

The ruler is 30 centimeters long.

1 Complete the number sentence. $30 \text{ cm} + $ _____ $\text{ cm} = $ _____ cm

2 How long is the string?   _____

Solve.

3 How long is the ribbon? Look at the
meter stick.

_____ centimeters

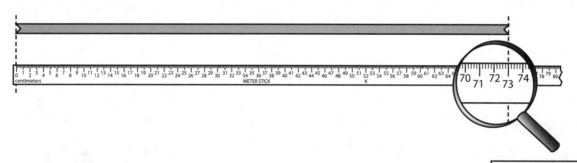

The meter stick
on this page is
not life-sized.

4 If you could measure an object using
a centimeter ruler or a meter stick, which
would you use? Why?

_____

_____

_____

5 Circle the objects that are easier to
measure with a centimeter ruler.
Underline the objects that are easier to
measure with a meter stick.

picnic table	crayon
toothbrush	piano
sofa	slice of bread

©Curriculum Associates, LLC   Copying is not permitted.

Name: _____

Measure Length

Solve the problems.

1 What is the length of the crayon?
Circle the correct answer.

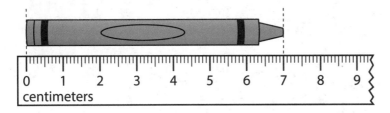

0 1 2 3 4 5 6 7 8 9
centimeters

What kind of ruler is being used to measure the crayon?

A 7 inches   **C** 6 centimeters

B 7 centimeters   **D** 6 inches

Glen chose **A**. This is wrong. How did Glen get his answer?

_____

_____

_____

_____

2 Layla started drawing the line above the ruler. Finish drawing the line to make it 2 inches long.

0 1 2 3
inches

Where on the ruler is the mark for 2 inches?

Solve.

3 Circle the objects that are easier to measure with a centimeter ruler. Underline the objects that are easier to measure with a meter stick.

park bench   stamp

paper clip   sandbox

4 Which piece of yarn is 4 centimeters long? Circle the correct answer.

A

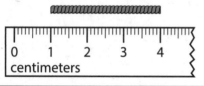

C

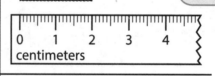

B

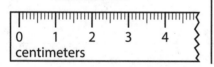

D

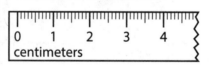

5 Jed wants to measure the length of the classroom chalkboard in inches. Which tool could he use? Circle all the correct answers.

A tape measure   **C** meter stick

B yardstick   **D** inch ruler

Dear Family,

This week your child is exploring using different units to measure the length of an object.

An object can be measured using many different units of length, such as inches, centimeters, or other objects.

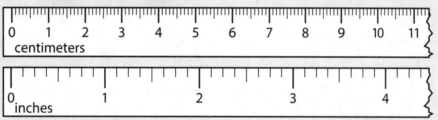

The toy fire truck is 5 centimeters long.
The toy fire truck is about 2 inches long.

It takes fewer inches than centimeters to measure the fire truck. An inch is longer than a centimeter, so you need fewer of them to measure an object. A centimeter is shorter than an inch, so you need more of them to measure an object.

Invite your child to share what he or she knows about measuring length with different units by doing the following activity together.

Materials: ruler, coins, household objects

- Play the following game with your child to help him or her see the results of measuring with longer or shorter units.
  - Have your child pick an object to measure.
  - Give your child a choice between measuring in inches, centimeters, pennies, or quarters. (Other small items like crackers or blocks can be used to measure.)
  - Choose one of the remaining units for yourself.
  - Measure the object together, once for each unit. Measure to the nearest whole unit.
  - Whoever needed fewer units to measure the object is the winner.
- Use the table to keep track of your data.

	Player 1	Player 2
Object		
Unit		
Measurement		

- Tell your child that you pick centimeters to measure the object. Ask your child which unit they could pick in order to win the game. Test your child's answer by playing again.

> If I choose to measure with centimeters, what unit would you pick to beat me?

Understand
Measurement With Different Units

Name: _____

> **Prerequisite: How do you measure length with rulers that have different units?**

Study the example showing how to measure length with a ruler. Then solve Problems 1–5.

Example

What is the length of the key in inches?

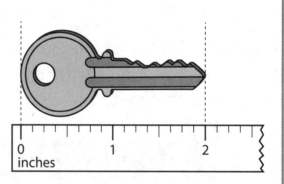

- Make sure one edge of the key is lined up at 0 on the ruler.

- Read the number lined up with the other edge of the key.

- Check the unit on the ruler. It is inches. ⟶ The key is 2 inches long.

---

1 What is the length of the fork in inches? _____ inches

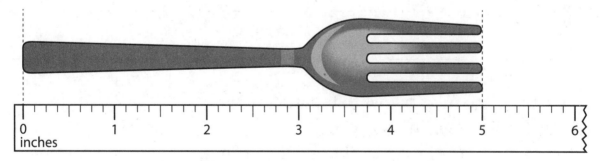

2 What is the length of the stick in centimeters? _____ centimeters

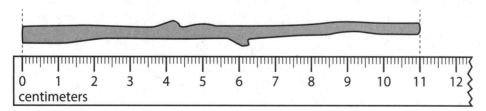

Solve.

3 How long is the leaf in centimeters?   _____ centimeters

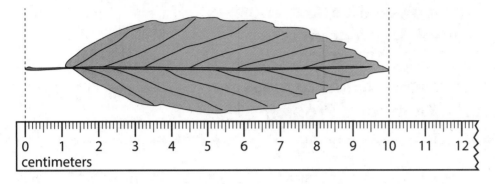

4 Chaz used the ruler below to measure a crayon. He says the crayon has a length of 3 centimeters. What did Chaz do wrong?

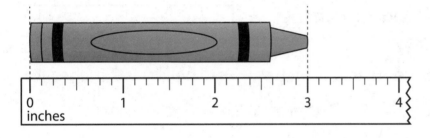

_____

_____

5 Lexi used the ruler below to measure the hair clip. She says the hair clip is 6 centimeters long. What did Lexi do wrong?

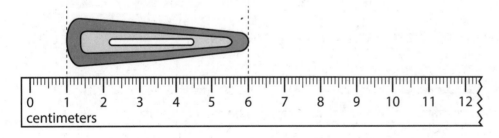

_____

Lesson 18 Understand Measurement With Different Units   ©Curriculum Associates, LLC   Copying is not permitted.

Name: _____

Compare Units of Measure

Study the example showing how to measure an object in inches and centimeters. Then solve Problems 1–8.

Example

How long is the ribbon in centimeters and in inches?

It is 5 centimeters long.

It is about 2 inches long.

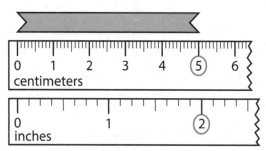

Inches are longer than centimeters. So it takes fewer inches to measure the length of the ribbon.

Use this pencil for Problems 1 and 2.

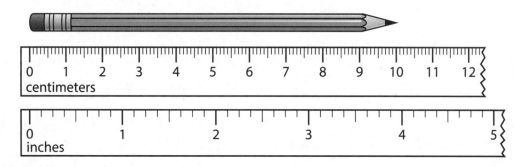

1 The pencil is _____ centimeters long.

2 The pencil is about _____ inches long.

3 Does it take fewer centimeters or inches to measure the length of the pencil? Why?

_____

_____

Lesson 18 Understand Measurement With Different Units   **191**

Solve.

Use this crayon for Problems 4 and 5.

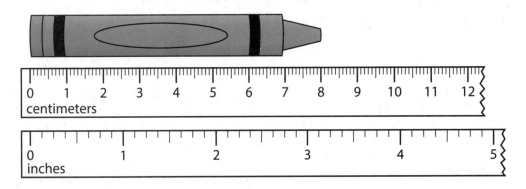

4 The crayon is _____ centimeters long.

5 The crayon is about _____ inches long.

6 Does it take more centimeters or inches to measure the length of the crayon? Why?

_____

_____

7 Would it take fewer glue sticks or pennies to measure the length of a book? Circle the correct answer.

8 Would it take more spoons or hair clips to measure the length of a table? Circle the correct answer.

Name: _____

Reason and Write

Look at the example. Underline a part that you think makes it a good answer.

Example

Rita measures the length of a marker.

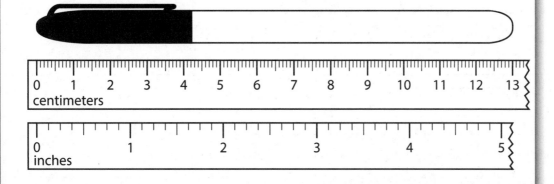

Which unit do you need more of to measure the length of Rita's marker?

Circle the correct answer.

(centimeters)   inches

Explain your answer.

Possible explanation: A centimeter is shorter than an inch. You need more centimeters than inches to measure the same length.

Where does the example . . .
- answer the question about units?
- explain the answer?

Lesson 18 Understand Measurement With Different Units   **193**

Solve the problem. Use what you learned from the example.

Adar measures the length of a bookmark.

Which unit do you need fewer of to measure the length of Adar's bookmark?

Circle the correct answer.

centimeters   inches

Explain your answer.

_____

_____

_____

_____

Did you . . .
- answer the question about units?
- explain the answer?

Dear Family,

This week your child is exploring estimating lengths of objects using benchmark objects.

estimate: use math thinking to make a close guess.

If you know the length of a common object, you can use that length to estimate the length of other objects.

Here are some helpful benchmarks you can use with your child to estimate length.

1 centimeter	1 inch	1 foot	1 meter or 1 yard
About the width of your little finger.	About the width of a quarter.	About the height of a math book.	About the width of a door.

To estimate the length of this ribbon, your child might compare it to quarters, and estimate that it would take 5 quarters to measure the ribbon, so it is about 5 inches long.

Invite your child to share what he or she knows about estimating length by doing the following activity together.

Estimating Length Activity

Materials: quarter, ruler, toys, or household objects

- Have your child collect three of his or her favorite small toys.

- Work with your child to estimate the length of each toy in centimeters. Encourage your child to use his or her little finger as a benchmark measurement of 1 centimeter.

- Estimate the length of the toy in inches, using a quarter as a benchmark measurement of 1 inch.

- Fill in the table below with the estimates. Then use a ruler to measure the toys' lengths to the nearest inch or centimeter.

- Ask your child which of his or her estimates was closest to the actual length.

	Centimeters		Inches	
	Estimate	Actual	Estimate	Actual
Toy #1				
Toy #2				
Toy #3				

Keep an eye open for examples of benchmark lengths in your everyday life. Share these with your child. For example, the height of a tree might be a good example of 20 feet, and the length of a sidewalk square might be a good example of 1 yard.

Prerequisite: How do you order objects by length?

Study the example showing how to compare and order objects by length. Then solve Problems 1–8.

Example

- Circle the shortest pencil.

- Draw an X on the longest pencil.

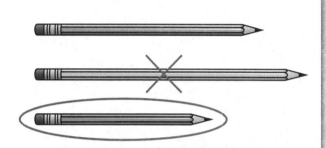

Circle the word that makes the sentence below true.

The top pencil is **longer / shorter** than the middle pencil.

Use the crayons for Problems 1–3.

1 Circle the shortest crayon.

2 Draw an X on the longest crayon.

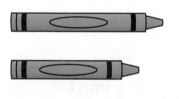

3 Circle the word that makes the sentence below true.

The top crayon is **longer / shorter** than the middle crayon.

Solve.

Use the bats for Problems 4–6.

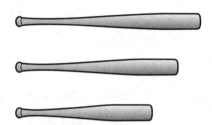

4 Circle the shortest bat.

5 Draw an X on the longest bat.

6 Circle the word that makes the sentence below true.

The bottom bat is **longer / shorter** than the middle bat.

7 Draw a line that is longer than both rectangles.

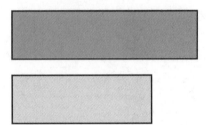

8 Draw a line that is shorter than both spoons.

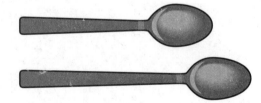

Name: _____

Use Different Units to Estimate Length

Study the example showing how to estimate length. Then solve Problems 1–8.

Example

Use the paper clip to estimate the length of the yarn.

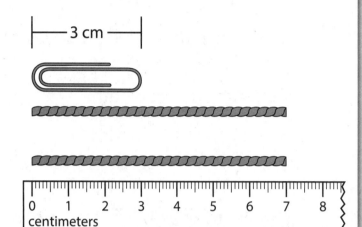

├─ 3 cm ─┤

- It looks like about 2 paper clips would fit above the yarn.
  Estimate: about 6 cm

Then use the ruler to measure the actual length of the yarn.
Actual length: 7 cm

---

1 Use the eraser to estimate the length of the marker.

├─ 1 inch ─┤

The marker is about _____ inches long.

2 Use the ruler to find the actual length of the marker.

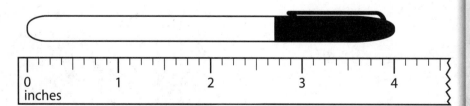

What is the actual length?
_____ inches

Vocabulary

to estimate use math thinking to make a close guess.

estimate a close guess made using math thinking.

Lesson 19 Understand Estimating Length   **199**

Solve.

3 Use the width of your little finger to estimate the length of the sticker.

The sticker is about _____ cm long.

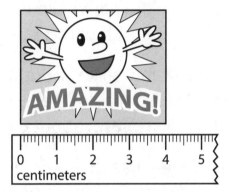

4 Use the centimeter ruler to measure the length of the sticker.

What is the actual length? _____ cm

5 Estimate the height of your front door in feet.

_____ feet

6 Estimate the length of a wall in your home in meters.

_____ meters

7 Which is the best estimate for the length of a park bench?

10 inches   24 meters   2 yards

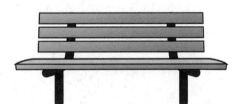

8 Which is the best estimate for the length of a piano keyboard?

12 inches   5 feet   20 yards

Reason and Write

Look at the example. Underline a part that you think makes it a good answer.

Example

Mrs. Chen made a list of lengths.

Mrs. Chen's List

Item	Length
unsharpened pencil	19 centimeters
sticky note	3 inches
egg carton	1 foot
height of door	2 meters

A. Choose an object in your home that is not on the list.

B. Estimate the length of the object you chose. Think about an item from Mrs. Chen's list to help you make your estimate.

C. Explain how you made your estimate.

Object: ____poster____   Estimate: ____3 feet____

Explain.

I thought about the egg carton from Mrs. Chen's list. The length of an egg carton is 1 foot. My poster looks as long as about 3 egg cartons. 1 + 1 + 1 = 3, so the poster is about 3 feet long.

Where does the example . . .

• tell the object that was chosen?

• show the estimate?

• explain which item from Mrs. Chen's list was used for help?

• explain how the estimate was made?

Solve the problem. Use what you learned from the example.

Mrs. Chen made a list of lengths.

Mrs. Chen's List

Item	Length
unsharpened pencil	19 centimeters
sticky note	3 inches
egg carton	1 foot
height of door	2 meters

A. Choose an object in your home that is not on the list.

B. Estimate the length of the object you chose. Think about an item from Mrs. Chen's list to help you make your estimate.

C. Explain how you made your estimate.

Object: _____ Estimate: _____

Explain.

_____

_____

_____

_____

_____

Where did you...
- write the object you chose?
- write your estimate?
- explain which item from Mrs. Chen's list you thought about to help you?
- explain how you made your estimate?

Dear Family,

This week your child is learning to compare measurements and find the difference in lengths.

Your child might see a question like this one: Troy and Gus measure their pencils. How much longer is Gus's pencil?

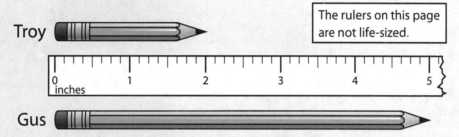

> The rulers on this page are not life-sized.

To find how much longer one pencil is than the other, find the difference between the lengths of the pencils. Gus's pencil is 5 inches long and Troy's is 2 inches long.

Since $5 - 3 = 2$, you know Gus's pencil is 3 inches longer than Troy's pencil.

You can also simply measure the difference.

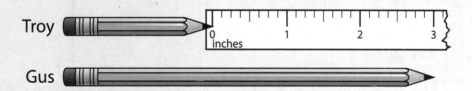

Invite your child to share what he or she knows about comparing length by doing the following activity together.

Comparing Lengths Activity

Materials: ruler, uncooked spaghetti (or strips of paper)

Play the following game with your child to practice comparing lengths.

- Hold one end of a piece of uncooked spaghetti and have your child hold the other end.

- Break the spaghetti into two pieces.

- Compare the lengths to determine who has the longer piece.

- Help your child measure both pieces of spaghetti in centimeters and find the difference. (Measure all objects to the nearest centimeter. Explain to your child that means that if the length of an object falls between two centimeter measurements, pick the one that is closer to the length of the object.)

- The person with the longer piece gets 1 point for each centimeter of difference. (So, a difference of 3 cm = 3 points). Record the winner's points in the table.

- Play the game two more times.

- Ask your child to add up the points to determine who won the game.

	Player A	Player B
Game 1		
Game 2		
Game 3		
Total		

Compare Lengths

Name: _____

Study the example showing how to use a third object to compare length. Then solve Problems 1–4.

Example

Use the paper strip to compare the lengths of the marker and the pencil.

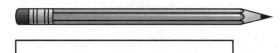

The marker is shorter than the paper strip.

The pencil is longer than the paper strip.

So the pencil is longer than the marker.

1   Michael used the same piece of yarn to compare the lengths of a stick and a baseball bat.

For each sentence, write *shorter* or *longer*.

a. The stick is _____ than the yarn.

b. The bat is _____ than the yarn.

c. That means the stick is _____ than the bat.

Solve.

2 Janelle used a crayon to compare the lengths of a leaf and a shell.

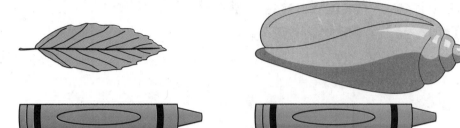

For each sentence, write *shorter* or *longer*.

a. The leaf is _____ than the crayon.

b. The shell is _____ than the crayon.

c. That means the leaf is _____ than the shell.

3 Manny used a ribbon to compare the lengths of a toy car and a mini football.

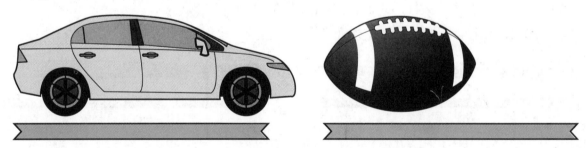

Write *shorter* or *longer*.

The toy car is _____ than the football.

4 Explain how you know which object in Problem 3 is shorter.

_____

_____

Name: _____

Find the Difference Between Lengths

Study the example showing how to find the difference between two lengths. Then solve Problems 1–8.

Example

How much longer is the gray hair clip than the green hair clip?

Write a number sentence.

$3 + ? = 5$ or $5 - 3 = ?$

The gray hair clip is 2 centimeters longer.

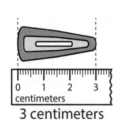
3 centimeters

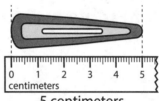
5 centimeters

The rulers in the Example are not life-sized.

1   Write the length of each ribbon.

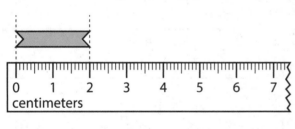

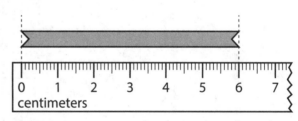

_____ centimeters   _____ centimeters

2   Complete the number sentence to compare the lengths.

_____ + ? = _____ and _____ − _____ = ?

3   How much longer is the gray ribbon than the green one?

_____ centimeters

Solve.

4 How much longer is the large paper clip than the shorter paper clip?

Show your work.

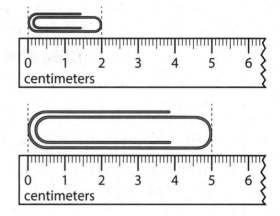

Answer: _____ centimeters

Use these pencils for Problems 5 to 8.

Aruna measured a green pencil and a gray pencil using a centimeter ruler.

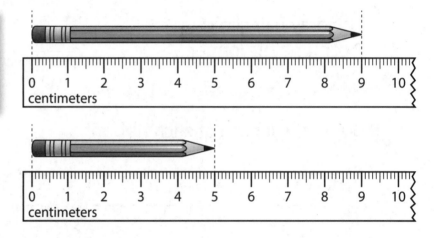

5 What is the length of the green pencil?   _____ centimeters

6 What is the length of the gray pencil?   _____ centimeters

7 Write a number sentence you can use to find the difference in lengths.   _____

8 How much longer is the green pencil than the gray pencil?   _____ centimeters

Name: _____

Ways to Find the Difference Between Lengths

Study the example showing two ways to find the difference between lengths. Then solve Problems 1–4.

Example

How much shorter is the paper clip than the pencil?

Measure each object.
- Pencil: 4 inches
- Paper clip: 1 inch
- $4 - 1 = ?$ or $1 + ? = 4$

Or measure the difference.
- Line up the two objects.
- Measure the difference.

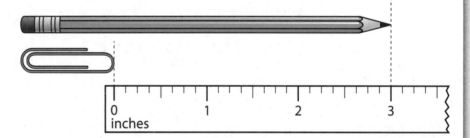

The paper clip is 3 inches shorter than the pencil.

1 How many inches shorter is the crayon than the marker?

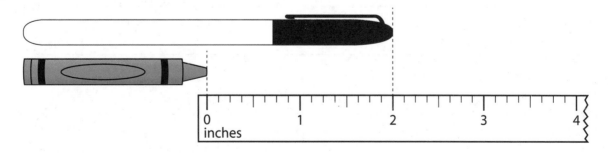

The crayon is _____ inches shorter than the marker.

Solve.

2 How much longer is the crayon than the paper clip?

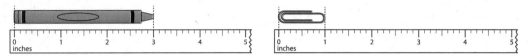

The crayon is _____ inches longer than the paper clip.

3 How much shorter is the eraser than the pen?

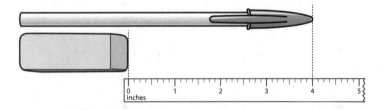

The eraser is _____ inches shorter than the pen.

The rulers on this page are not life-sized.

4 Do you like the method shown in Problem 2 or in Problem 3 better? Explain why.

_____

_____

_____

Name: _____

Compare Lengths

Solve the problems.

1 What is the difference in the lengths of the two pieces of yarn? The ruler shows centimeters.

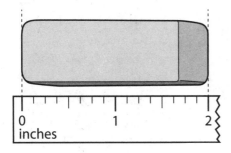

Show your work.

Answer: _____

Remember, finding the difference in length means you tell how much longer or shorter one piece of yarn is than the other.

2 How much longer is the eraser than the paper clip? Circle the correct answer.

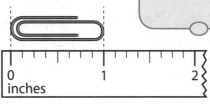

What number sentence can you write to help you find the answer?

A 1 inch   **C** 3 inches

B 2 inches   **D** 4 inches

Jane chose **C**. This is wrong. How did Jane get her answer?

_____

_____

Solve.

3 Frank drew the line below. Draw a line below it that is 3 centimeters shorter.

How many centimeters long should your line be?

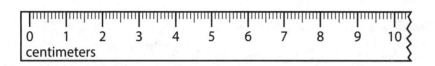

0 1 2 3 4 5 6 7 8 9 10
centimeters

4 Keith's jump rope is 84 inches long. Ruby's jump rope is 96 inches long. What number sentence could you use to find out how much longer Ruby's jump rope is? Circle all the correct answers.

Can you use a bar model to help you decide which number sentences you could use?

A $96 + 84 = ?$ **C** $84 + ? = 96$

B $84 - 96 = ?$ **D** $96 - 84 = ?$

5 Sadie says the marker is 1 inch longer than the pencil. What did Sadie do wrong?

What do you need to do first when you measure the difference?

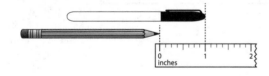

0 1 2
inches

_____

_____

_____

The ruler for this problem is not life-sized.

Dear Family,

This week your child is learning to solve one- and two-step word problems involving length.

Your child might see a problem like this: Dallas has a new jump rope that is 96 inches long. Her jump rope is made of three different colored sections: green, blue, and pink. The green section is 39 inches long. The blue section is 34 inches long. How long is the pink section?

First, model the problem to organize the information.

bar model

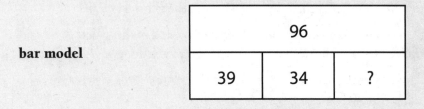

open number line

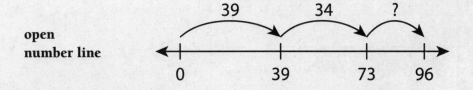

Then, write and solve number sentences based on one of the models.

How long is the green and blue sections combined?
39 + 34 = 73
How much more rope is there?
73 + ? = 96 or 96 − 73 = ?
73 + 23 = 96 and 96 − 73 = 23
The pink section is 23 inches.

Invite your child to share what he or she knows about solving one- and two-step measurement word problems by doing the following activity together.

NEXT

Adding and Subtracting Lengths Activity

Materials: yardstick or tape measure

Select several objects from around the house and measure their heights to the nearest inch. Record in the table below. Make up and solve addition and subtraction word problems with your child.

Examples:

- How much taller is the refrigerator than the table?

- If the desk was 2 inches taller, how tall would it be?

- If I stacked a book and a lamp on the desk, how tall would the stack be?

- How much taller is the tallest chair than the shortest chair?

- If I stacked two chairs in the doorway, how tall is the space between the top of the chairs and the top of the doorway?

Object	Height (in inches)

Remember to measure everything in inches, not in feet.

Add and Subtract Lengths

Name: _____

Study the example showing how to compare two lengths. Then solve Problems 1–6.

Example

How much shorter is the gray ribbon than the green ribbon?

Write a number sentence.

$6 - 2 = ?$ or $2 + ? = 6$

The gray ribbon is 4 inches shorter.

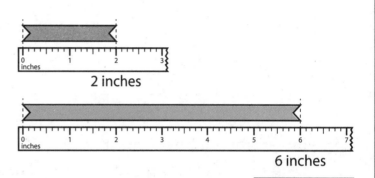

2 inches

6 inches

The rulers in the Example are not life-sized.

---

1   Write the length of each paper clip.

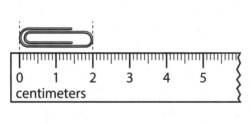

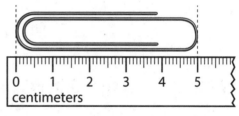

_____ centimeters   _____ centimeters

2   Complete the number sentence to compare the lengths.

_____ + ? = _____ and _____ − _____ = ?

3   How much longer is the large paper clip than the small one?

_____ centimeters

Solve.

4 How many centimeters longer is the eraser than the paper clip?

Show your work.

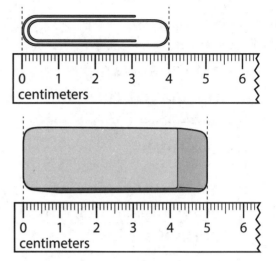

Answer: _____

5 How many inches shorter is the gray yarn than the green yarn?

Show your work.

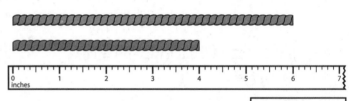

This ruler is not life-sized.

Answer: _____

6 What is the difference in the lengths of the ropes? The tape measure below them shows feet.

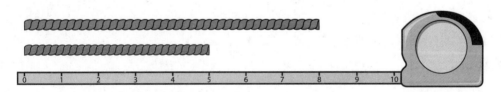

This tape measure is not life-sized.

Show your work.

Answer: _____

Name: _____

Solve Problems About Length

Study the example showing how to solve a problem about length. Then solve Problems 1–7.

Example

Judy has a ribbon 43 centimeters long. She cuts off 6 centimeters. How long is the ribbon now?

- Make a bar model.
- Write a number sentence.
- Use a number line.

The ribbon is now 37 centimeters long.

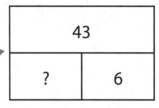

$$43 - 6 = ? \quad \text{or} \quad ? + 6 = 43$$

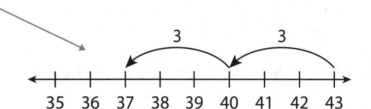

Marie kicked a ball 68 feet. Liam kicked a ball that went 17 feet less than that. How far did Liam kick the ball?

1 Fill in the two empty boxes in the bar model to show this problem.

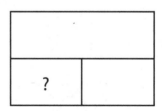

2 Complete the number sentences.

$68 -$ _____ $= ?$ $? +$ _____ $= 68$

3 How far did Liam kick the ball? _____

Solve.

4 Ms. Rom puts together two hoses. One hose is 24 meters long. When she puts the hoses together, they are 76 meters long.

Complete the number sentences to help Ms. Rom find the length of the other hose.

_____ − 24 = ?   24 + ? = _____

5 In Problem 4, what is the length of the other hose?

_____

6 Mr. Becker builds a fence that is 14 feet long. Mrs. Vega builds a fence 37 feet long. How much shorter is Mr. Becker's fence than Mrs. Vega's fence?

Show your work.

Answer: _____

7 Jackson has a piece of yarn that is 89 centimeters long. He cuts off 19 centimeters to make it the right length for a craft project. How long is the piece of yarn now?

Show your work.

Answer: _____

Name: _____

Solve Two-Step Problems About Length

Study the example showing how to solve a two-step problem about length. Then solve Problems 1–7.

Example

Fay makes a paper chain that is 34 inches long. Liz makes a paper chain that is 6 inches longer than Fay's. They put their chains together. How long is the paper chain now?

- Make a bar model.
- Write a number sentence.

The paper chain is now 74 inches long.

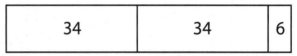

| 34 | 34 | 6 |

$$34 + 34 + 6$$
$$34 + 40 = 74$$

---

1 Fill in the boxes on the number line to model the Example.

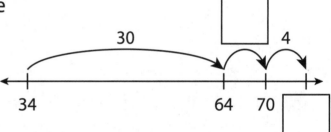

Lester makes a string of beads 17 inches long. Jill makes a string of beads that is 3 inches longer than Lester's. They put their strings together.

2 Complete the number sentence to find the total length of the string of beads.

$$17 + \underline{} = ?$$

3 How long is the string of beads now?

_____ inches

Solve.

4 Olga has 13 meters of ribbon. She uses 4 meters. Then she uses 2 meters.

Complete the number sentences below to help Olga find out how much ribbon she has left.

13 − _____ = 9 and 9 − 2 = _____

5 In Problem 4, how much ribbon is left?

_____ meters

6 Raj has a paper strip that is 19 inches long. He uses 5 inches. Then he uses 6 inches. How much of the paper strip is left?

Show your work.

Answer: _____

7 Al wants his toy train tracks to be 30 inches long. Al has one track that is 12 inches long. He has another track that is 3 inches longer than the first one. Together, are these two tracks long enough? Explain.

Show your work.

_____

_____

Name: _____

Add and Subtract Lengths

Solve the problems.

1 Mina had 11 yards of ribbon. She used 3 yards to tie onto balloons and 2 yards to wrap presents. How much ribbon is left? Circle the correct answer.

A 16 yards   **C** 8 yards

B 14 yards   **D** 6 yards

Dennis chose **A**. This is wrong. How did Dennis get his answer?

_____

_____

_____

_____

To find how much is left, should you add or subtract the ribbon that Mina uses?

2 Stu's block tower is 39 inches tall. Jen's block tower is 17 inches shorter than Stu's. How tall is Jen's block tower?

Which number sentences can you use to solve the problem? Circle all the correct answers.

A $39 - ? = 17$ **C** $17 + 39 = ?$

B $39 - 17 = ?$ **D** $17 + ? = 39$

Can you use a model to help you solve the problem?

Solve.

3 Ed has two dog leashes. The purple leash is 84 inches long. The red leash is 75 inches long. How much shorter is the red leash?

When you compare you find the difference.

Show your work.

Answer: _____

4 Anjali crossed a playground that was 45 meters long. First she walked for 5 meters. Then she skipped for 23 meters. She ran the rest of the way. How many meters did Anjali run?

After Anjali walked 5 meters, how much of the playground did she have left to cross?

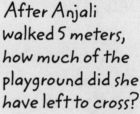

Circle all the number sentences that show a step in solving the problem.

A $45 + 5 = ?$ **C** $23 + 45 = ?$

B $45 - 5 = ?$ **D** $40 - 23 = ?$

5 Ms. Bard uses 24 centimeters of thread to sew a button. Then she uses 31 centimeters of thread to sew another button. She has 9 centimeters of thread left. How much thread did Ms. Bard start with?

To find the amount Ms. Bard started with, should you add or subtract the amount she used?

Show your work.

Answer: _____

Dear Family,

This week your child is exploring how to organize a set of measurements using a line plot.

Here is a table showing the lengths of four crayons. A line plot can show how many crayons of each length there are.

Crayon	Length (inches)
A	3
B	2
C	4
D	2

A **line plot** is made up of a number line, a title, and a label that tells what is being shown. It has an X for each measurement.

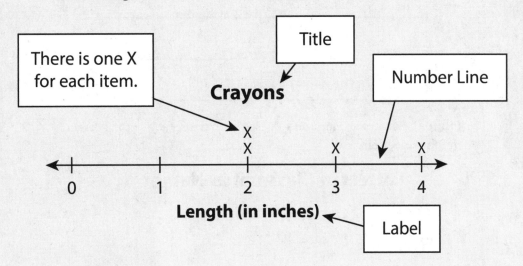

Invite your child to share what he or she knows about line plots by doing the following activity together.

Together make a line plot of the number of letters in the first names of several of your child's classmates.

- First gather the data. Choose up to six classmates and count the number of letters in each name.

- Organize the data in the table below.

Name	Number of Letters

- Fill in the line plot. Mark one "X" for each name, above the correct number of letters.

Letters in Classmates' Names

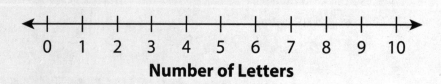

0 1 2 3 4 5 6 7 8 9 10

Number of Letters

- Ask your child how the line plot would change if you added in the names Dan, Jon, and Sam.

Name: _____

Prerequisite: How can you make tally charts?

Study the example showing how to make a tally chart. Then solve Problems 1–4.

Example

How many of each kind of sticker are there? Complete the tally chart.

• Draw one tally mark for each sticker.

• You can cross out each sticker after you count it to keep track.

Sticker	How Many
☺	|||
☆	✝✝✝| I
☾	||

---

1 How many of each kind of ball are there? Complete the tally chart.

Ball	How Many
⚽	
🏈	
🏀	

Solve.

2 How many are there of each kind of classroom tool? Complete the tally chart.

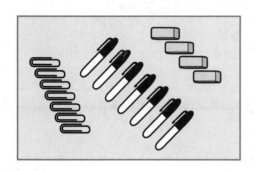

Classroom Tool	How Many
✏️	
📎	
▭	

3 How many are there of each shape? Complete the tally chart.

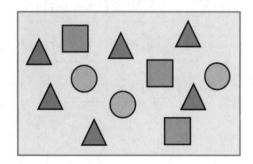

Shape	How Many
▲	
■	
●	

4 Sam measured the lengths of 10 leaves. He wrote this list. Complete the tally chart to show the data.

Leaf Lengths
2 inches
6 inches
2 inches
5 inches
2 inches
4 inches
4 inches
3 inches

Length	How Many
1 inch	
2 inches	
3 inches	
4 inches	
5 inches	
6 inches	
7 inches	

Name: _____

Read and Make Line Plots

Study the example showing how to read a line plot. Then solve Problems 1–9.

Example

Kyle measured each leaf in his collection using centimeters. He made this line plot.

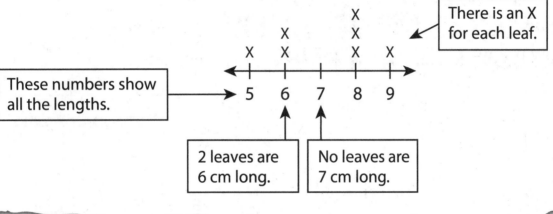

Leaf Lengths (in centimeters)

There is an X for each leaf.

These numbers show all the lengths.

2 leaves are 6 cm long.

No leaves are 7 cm long.

1 What is the length of the shortest leaf?

_____5_____ centimeters

2 What is the length of the longest leaf?

_____9_____ centimeters

3 How many leaves are 8 centimeters long?

_____3_____

4 How many leaves are in Kyle's collection?

_____7_____

Solve.

Rita measured the ribbons in her craft box. The ribbons and their lengths are shown below.

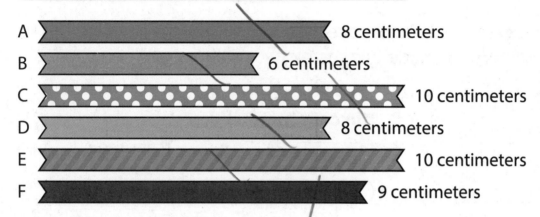

A 8 centimeters

B 6 centimeters

C 10 centimeters

D 8 centimeters

E 10 centimeters

F 9 centimeters

5 What is the length of ribbon A?

_____ centimeters

6 Draw an X above that number on the line plot.

7 For each of the other ribbons, draw an X on the line plot.

8 What is the length of the shortest ribbon?

_____ centimeters

9 How many ribbons are longer than 8 centimeters?

_____

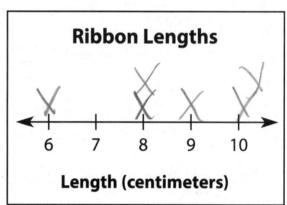

Ribbon Lengths

6   7   8   9   10

Length (centimeters)

Name: _____

Understanding and Reading Line Plots

Look at the example. Underline a part that you think makes it a good answer.

Example

Lexi measures the lengths of her toy cars. The lengths are shown in the table. Use the lengths to make a line plot.

Toy Car	Length (inches)
A	4
B	3
C	7
D	5
E	3
F	5

1. Write a title for the line plot.

2. Fill in the numbers for length on the line plot.

3. Draw an X on the line plot for each toy car.

4. Answer the question below the line plot.

Toy Car Lengths

```
X           X
X     X     X           X
←——+——+——+——+——+——→
┌───┬───┬───┬───┬───┐
│ 3 │ 4 │ 5 │ 6 │ 7 │
└───┴───┴───┴───┴───┘
```

Length (inches)

> Where does the example...
> • write a title for the line plot?
> • write numbers on the line plot?
> • use Xs to show the car lengths?
> • answer the question?

How did you decide which number should go in each box below the number line? Explain.

I wrote the numbers from the chart in order, starting with the smallest number. I only wrote each number once. I included 6 even though no cars are 6 inches long. That is because you have to include all the numbers that are between the smallest and largest numbers.

Lesson 22 Understand Reading and Making Line Plots   **229**

Solve the problem. Use what you learned from the example.

Paco measures the lengths of the bookmarks he has in his desk. The lengths are shown in the chart. Use the lengths to make a line plot.

Bookmark	Length (inches)
A	8
B	7
C	4
D	6
E	7
F	4

1. Write a title for the line plot.

2. Fill in the numbers for length on the line plot.

3. Draw an X on the line plot for each bookmark.

4. Answer the question below the line plot.

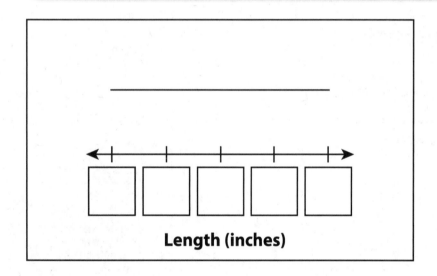

Length (inches)

Did you . . .

• write a title for the line plot?

• write numbers on the line plot?

• use Xs to show the bookmark lengths?

• answer the question?

How did you decide where to draw the Xs on the number line? Explain.

_____

_____

_____

_____

Dear Family,

This week your child is learning about picture graphs and bar graphs.

> **data:** a set of collected information.
> **picture graph:** a way to show data using pictures.
> **bar graph:** a way to show data using rectangular bars.

This **picture graph** shows the number of sunny, rainy, cloudy, and snowy days last week. Each symbol represents 1 day.

Weather Last Week

Sunny	☀ ☀ ☀
Rainy	🌧
Cloudy	☁ ☁
Snowy	❄

This **bar graph** shows the favorite fruits of 10 friends. The height of each bar tells how many friends prefer each type of fruit.

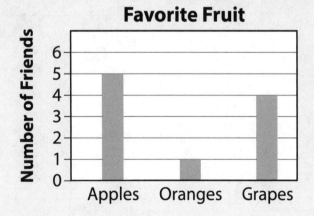

Invite your child to share what he or she knows about graphs by doing the following activity together.

Graph Activity

Materials: coins, paper, markers

Practice making a picture graph and a bar graph with your child.

- Gather 10–12 different coins.

- Have your child sort the pennies, nickels, dimes, and quarters, and count the number of each type of coin.

- Fill in the picture graph and the bar graph with the data. Draw circles with the letters *P*, *N*, *D*, and *Q* to show coins on the picture graph.

- Ask your child to describe the differences between the two graphs, which type he or she prefers, and why.

Coins

Pennies	
Nickels	
Dimes	
Quarters	

Coins

```
10 —————————————————————
 9 —————————————————————
 8 —————————————————————
 7 —————————————————————
 6 —————————————————————
 5 —————————————————————
 4 —————————————————————
 3 —————————————————————
 2 —————————————————————
 1 —————————————————————
 0 —
     Pennies  Nickels  Dimes  Quarters
```

Draw and Use Bar Graphs and Picture Graphs

Name: _____

Study the example showing how to use information in picture graphs. Then solve Problems 1–9.

Example

Tess made this picture graph to show the kinds of shoes her friends are wearing. How many friends are wearing sneakers or sandals?

Types of Shoes

Sneakers	☺☺☺☺☺☺☺
Boots	☺☺
Sandals	☺☺☺☺☺

7 friends are wearing sneakers.

5 friends are wearing sandals.

$7 + 5 = 12$

So, 12 friends are wearing sneakers or sandals.

Use the picture graph in the Example to answer the problems below.

1 How many friends are wearing sandals?

_____

2 How many friends are wearing boots?

_____

3 Complete the number sentence to show how many more friends are wearing sandals than boots.

$5 - 2 =$ _____

Vocabulary

picture graph
a way to show data using pictures.

Solve.

Ezra asked his friends if they like to draw with crayons, pencils, or markers best. Then he made this picture graph.

Favorite Drawing Tools

Crayons	☺ ☺ ☺ ☺ ☺ ☺
Pencils	☺ ☺ ☺ ☺ ☺ ☺ ☺ ☺
Markers	☺ ☺ ☺

4 How many friends chose pencils? _____

5 How many friends chose markers? _____

6 Complete the number sentence to show how many fewer friends chose markers than pencils.

$8 - 3 =$ _____

7 Write a number sentence to show how many friends chose crayons or markers.

_____ + _____ = _____

8 Do more friends like to draw with crayons or pencils? Circle what more friends like. Then write how many more friends like to draw with that tool.

Crayons

Pencils

_____ more

9 Write another question about the picture graph. Then answer your question.

_____

_____

Name: _____

Use a Picture Graph and Bar Graph

Study the example showing how to use a picture graph and a bar graph. Then solve Problems 1–13.

Example

Val counted the shapes of her stickers. She made a bar graph. How many of her stickers are circles?

The bar for Circles goes up to the line for 6.

Val has 6 circle stickers.

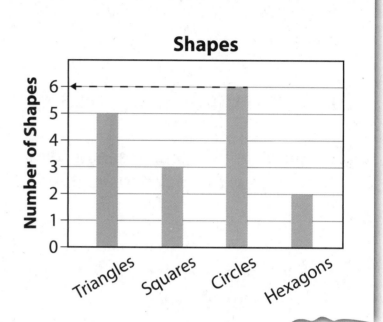

Shapes

Use the information from the Example to answer Problems 1–4.

1 How many triangles does Val have? __5__

2 How many hexagons does Val have? __2__

A+

3 Complete the number sentence to show how many more triangles than hexagons Val has.

5 − __2__ = __3__

4 Write a number sentence to show how many squares and circles Val has in all.

_____ + _____ = _____

Vocabulary

bar graph a way to show data using bars.

Solve.

Saul asked his friends, "What is your favorite fruit?" Then he made this picture graph.

Favorite Fruits

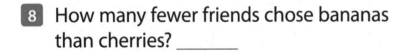

5 How many friends chose apples? _____

6 How many friends chose pears? _____

7 Complete the number sentence to show how many friends chose apples or pears.

   7 + _____ = _____

8 How many fewer friends chose bananas than cherries? _____

Rachel asked her friends, "What is your favorite instrument?" Then she made this bar graph.

Favorite Instruments

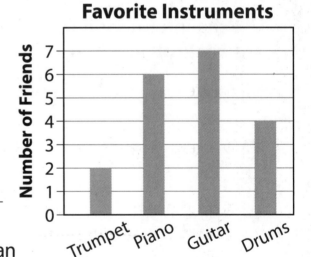

9 How many friends chose piano? _____

10 How many friends chose drums? _____

11 How many more friends chose piano than drums? _____

12 How many fewer friends chose trumpet than guitar? _____

13 How many friends did Rachel ask? _____

Name: _____

Make Bar Graphs and Picture Graphs

Study the example showing how to make a bar graph from a tally chart. Then solve Problems 1–8.

Example

Ava made the tally chart below to show the colors of heart stickers she has. Then she made the bar graph.

Yellow	Pink	Red

Ava wrote the title of her graph above it.

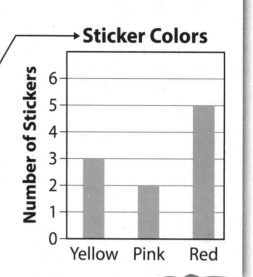

Sticker Colors

Ava wants to make a picture graph. Use the information in Ava's tally chart for Problems 1–4.

1 Write a title on the line above the graph.

2 Write the missing color name next to Yellow and Pink.

3 Draw the correct number of hearts above the word Yellow.

4 Draw the correct number of hearts above the word Pink.

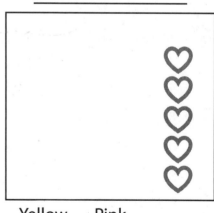

Solve.

Carter made this tally chart to show the colors of flowers in his window box. Use the data in Carter's tally chart to complete the bar graph.

White	Purple	Orange
IIII	IIII I	III

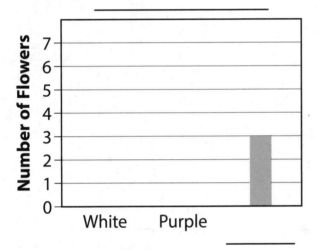

5 What is a good title for the graph? Write it on the line above the graph.

6 Fill in the missing color next to the word Purple.

7 Draw a bar to show how many white flowers there are.

8 Draw a bar to show how many purple flowers there are.

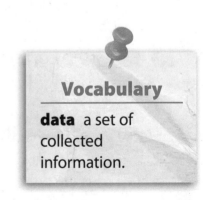

Vocabulary

data a set of collected information.

Dear Family,

This week your child is learning to tell time to the nearest five minutes.

For example, he or she is learning to tell what time this clock shows.

The short hand tells the hour. It's called the **hour hand**. It's pointing between the 5 and the 6. The hour is 5.

The long hand shows the minutes. It's called the **minute hand**. It's pointing to 7. Skip count by five 7 times to find how many minutes after five o'clock it is.

5, 10, 15, 20, 25, 30, 35

The time on the clock is 5:35, or 35 minutes after five o'clock.

Digital clocks show time using only numbers instead of hands. They also tell whether it is AM (midnight to noon) or PM (noon to midnight).

Invite your child to share what he or she knows about telling time by doing the following activity together.

Materials: two crayons of different lengths

Help your child learn to show time on a clock face with this activity.

- Have family members take turns naming their favorite time of day, such as breakfast, bed time, or arriving home.

- Ask your child to place the crayons as the hands on the clock below to show the time of day that each activity happens. Help by naming the times: for example, "I get home from work at 5:20" or "We eat dinner at 6:30."

- Next, place the hands on the clock to show other times, and ask your child to tell the time and describe something that happens at that time.

Tell and Write Time

Name: _____

**Study the example showing how to tell time.
Then solve Problems 1–6.**

Example

Circle the clock that shows **9:00**.

Say: **9 o'clock**

The hour hand points to 9.
The minute hand points to 12.
So this clock shows 9:00.

The hour hand points halfway
between 9 and 10. The minute
hand points to 6. So this clock
shows 9:30.

---

1 Circle the clock that shows 2:30.

2 Read the digital clock. Draw
the hands on the other clock
to show the same time.

Solve.

3 Circle the clock that shows 7:00.

4 Circle the clock that shows 3:30.

5 Read the digital clock. Draw the hands on the other clock to show the same time.

6 It is five o'clock. Fill in the correct time on the digital clock. Draw the time on the other clock.

5:0

Name: _____

Tell and Write Time

Study the example showing how to tell and write time. Then solve Problems 1–6.

Example

The first clock shows when Lil started eating dinner. Show the same time on a digital clock.

- The minute hand points to 4. So skip count by five 4 times to find the number of minutes.

- Dinner is in the evening. Draw a dot on the digital clock next to PM.

PM means the hours from noon to midnight.

---

1 Gino went on a picnic in the afternoon. The first clock shows when the picnic started. Show how the time would look on a digital clock. Be sure to mark AM or PM.

2 Nima's soccer team plays on Sunday mornings. Her first game started at the time shown on the digital clock. Draw the same time on the other clock.

Solve.

3 Bryce had a piano lesson after school. His lesson ended at the time shown on the digital clock. Draw the same time on the other clock.

4 The first clock shows when Nadya brushed her teeth before school. Show how the time would look on a digital clock. Be sure to mark AM or PM.

5 The first clock shows when Mr. Wade's class started recess. Show how the time would look on a digital clock. Be sure to mark AM or PM.

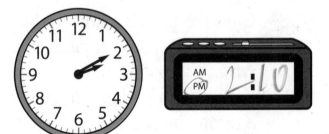

6 Eric called his aunt at 10:15 in the morning. Draw hands on the clock to show 10:15. Then write the time on the digital clock. Be sure to mark AM or PM.

Name: _____

Tell and Write Time

Solve the problems.

1 Luis gets home from school at 3:25. Which clock shows the time Luis gets home? Circle all the correct answers.

A   **B**   **C**   **D**

What two numbers will the hour hand be between? Should the digital clock show AM or PM?

2 Justin finishes art class at 2:40 in the afternoon. Draw hands on the clock to show 2:40. Then write the time on the digital clock. Be sure to mark AM or PM.

Is the hour hand or minute hand longer? How can you tell if the time is AM or PM?

3 Which number does the minute hand point to when a clock shows 5:10? Circle the correct answer.

A 10   **C** 3

B 5   **D** 2

Can you draw a picture to help you?

Solve.

4 Lita's mom wakes her up to get ready for school at the time shown on the clock.

Which digital clock shows the time Lita's mom wakes her up? Circle the correct answer.

Where does the hour hand point when it is almost the next hour?

A   B   C   D

5 Rory has dance class on Saturdays at the time shown on the clock. What time does Rory have dance class? Circle the correct answer.

Which hand tells the minutes?

A 3:09   C 9:15

B 3:45   D 9:30

Mike chose **B**. This is wrong. How did Mike get his answer?

he swapt the hands small hand was the minite hand and the long hand wos

©Curriculum Associates, LLC   Copying is not permitted.

Dear Family,

This week your child is learning about the names and values of coins and bills.

For example, your child might see a question like this: Aiden bought bread and cheese. He used these bills and coins to pay. How much did he spend?

First, count the number of dollars.

$1 $2 $3 $4

Then, count the coins.

25¢   50¢   75¢   85¢   95¢

Aiden spent 4 dollars and 95 cents.

Invite your child to share what he or she knows about money by doing the following activity together.

NEXT

Materials: flyers or catalogs that show prices for food, toys, or clothing; scissors; real money (optional)

- Together, choose a flyer. Let your child choose something that costs under $10.

- Help your child cut out the pictures below of the money needed for the purchase. If possible, use real money.

- Have your child "pay" by counting out the money.

Solve Word Problems Involving Money

Name: _____

Prerequisite: Count by 1, 2, and 5 on a 120 Chart

Study the example showing how to count by 1, 2, and 5 on a 120 chart. Then solve Problems 1–3.

Example

How can you count on the 120 chart?

Count by 2.   Count by 5.

21	22	23	24	25	26	27	28	29	30
31	32	33	34	35	36	37	38	39	40
41	42	43	44	45	46	47	48	49	50

Count by 1.

Fill in the blanks.

Count by 1: 46, _47_, _48_, 49, 50

Count by 2: 22, _24_, _26_, _28_, _30_, _32_, 34

Count by 5: 25, _30_, _35_, _40_, _45_, 50

---

1 Fill in the blanks. Use the chart.

91	92	93	94	95	96	97	98	99	100
101	102	103	104	105	106	107	108	109	110
111	112	113	114	115	116	117	118	119	120

Count by 1: 108, _____, 110, _____, 112, _____

Count by 2: 96, _____, _____, 102, _____, 106

Count by 5: 95, _____, 105, 110, _____, 120

Solve.

2 Fill in the blanks. Use the chart.

41	42	43	44	45	46	47	48	49	50
51	52	53	54	55	56	57	58	59	60
61	62	63	64	65	66	67	68	69	70

Count by 1: 49, _____, _____, _____, 53, _____, 55

Count by 2: 52, _____, 56, _____, _____, 62, _____

Count by 5: 40, 45, _____, _____, 60, _____

3 Fill in the blanks. Use the chart.

81	82	83	84	85	86	87	88	89	90
91	92	93	94	95	96	97	98	99	100
101	102	103	104	105	106	107	108	109	110

Count by 1: 95, _____, 97, _____, _____, 100, _____

Count by 2: 98, _____, _____, _____, _____, 108, _____

Count by 5: 85, _____, 95, _____, _____, 110

Name: _____

Find the Value of a Set of Coins

Study the example showing how to find the value of a set of coins. Then solve Problems 1–7.

Example

Mindy has these coins. How many cents does she have?

You can skip count.

25   35   45   55   60   **61**

Mindy has **61¢**.

You can add.

25 + 10 + 10 + 10 + 5 + 1

25   +   30   +   5 + 1 = **61¢**

---

1 Look at Grant's coins below. Use skip counting to find the total value of these coins. Fill in the blanks.

10¢, _____, 25¢, _____, _____, 36¢, _____

2 Look at Grant's coins in Problem 1. Add the values of the coins. Fill in the boxes.

10 + 10 + 5 + 5 + 5 + 1 + 1

☐ + 15 + ☐ = ☐ ¢

3 Look at Grant's coins in Problem 1. How many cents does Grant have?

_____ ¢

Solve.

4 Hart has these coins. How many cents does he have?

Show your work.

Answer: _____ ¢

5 Lila has these coins. How many cents does she have?

Show your work.

Answer: _____ ¢

6 Ted has these coins. How many cents does he have?

Show your work.

Answer: _____ ¢

7 Look at the coins in Problem 6. Draw another set of coins that is worth the same amount.

Draw your coins like this:
(25) (10) (5) (1)

Name: _____

Solve Word Problems Involving Money

Study the example showing how to solve a word problem involving money. Then solve Problems 1–7.

Example

Kit had $50. Jan had two $10 bills and two $5 bills. Jan earned more money raking leaves. Then she had the same amount of money as Kit. How much money did Jan earn raking leaves?

Step 1: Find how much money Jan had at the start. $\longrightarrow$ 10 + 10 + 5 + 5 = 30

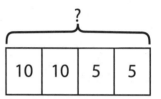

Step 2: Find how much money Jan earned raking. $\longrightarrow$ 50 − 30 = 20

Jan earned $20 raking leaves.

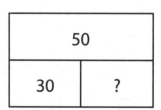

1 Show how you could use an open number line to model Step 1 of the Example. Write a number in each box.

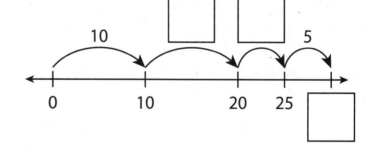

2 Show how you could use an open number line to model Step 2 of the Example. Write a number in the box.

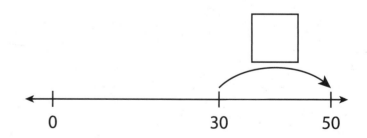

Solve.

Noah has two $20 bills and one $10 bill.
Thai has two $10 bills and two $5 bills.

3 Complete the number sentence to show
how much money Noah has. 20 + 20 + 10 = _____

4 Write a number sentence to show how
much money Thai has. _____ + _____ + _____ + _____ = _____

5 Who has less money? How much less?

_____

_____

Ivy has $75. Liz has three $20 bills and one
$5 bill. Liz gets more money recycling
cans. Then she has the same amount of
money as Ivy.

6 How much money does Liz get
recycling cans?

Show your work.

Answer: _____

7 Ivy has 6 bills. What bills could Ivy have?

_____

_____

_____

Name: _____

Solve Word Problems Involving Money

Solve the problems.

1 Circle *True* or *False* for each statement.

> Can you count by 5 or 10 to help you think about each statement?

a. One $10 bill is worth the same as two $5 bills.   True   False

b. One $20 bill is worth the same as two $10 bills.   True   False

c. Three $5 bills are worth the same as two $10 bills.   True   False

d. Four $5 bills are worth the same as two $10 bills.   True   False

2 Dave has two $20 bills and one $5 bill. Mac has three $5 bills and two $10 bills. Who has more money? How much more?

Show your work.

> How can you find the total value of Dave's bills? How can you find the total value of Mac's bills?

Answer: _____

3 What is the total value of these coins?

> You can use skip counting to help you solve.

Answer: _____ ¢

Solve.

4 A pencil costs 39¢. Zack uses two quarters to pay for it. Which coins could he get back in change? Circle all the correct answers.

What should Zack's change be worth?

A

B

C

D

5 Marcy has 27¢. Which could be Marcy's coins? Circle the correct answer.

You can touch each coin as you count it to help you keep track.

A

B

C

D

Leah chose **C**. This is wrong. How did Leah get her answer?

_____

_____

_____

Name: _____

Measure It

What you need: Recording Sheet, Measure It Game Cards, centimeter ruler

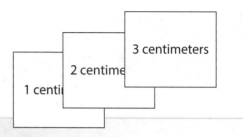

Directions

- Mix up the game cards. Put them face down in a pile.

- Take turns. On your turn, take the top card.

- Use a ruler to find the string with that length on your Recording Sheet. Write the length in the blank.

- Play until both players have 4 measurements.

- Add the lengths of all your string pieces. The player with the longest total length wins the game.

I measured a string that is only 1 centimeter long. That is the shortest one of all!

Measure It Recording Sheet

1. ▨▨▨▨▨▨▨▨▨▨▨▨▨▨▨   1. _____ centimeters

2. ▨▨▨▨▨▨   2. _____ centimeters

3. ▨▨▨▨▨▨▨▨▨▨▨▨▨▨▨▨▨▨▨   3. _____ centimeters

4. ▨▨▨▨▨▨▨▨▨   4. _____ centimeters

5. ▨▨▨   5. _____ centimeter

6. ▨▨▨▨▨▨▨   6. _____ centimeters

7. ▨▨▨▨▨▨▨▨▨▨▨▨▨▨   7. _____ centimeters

8. ▨▨▨   8. _____ centimeters

Total _____ + _____ + _____ + _____ = _____

The total length is _____ centimeters.

1 centimeter

2 centimeters

3 centimeters

5 centimeters

6 centimeters

8 centimeters

10 centimeters

12 centimeters

Measurement and Data

In this unit you learned to:	Lesson
use a ruler to measure an object.	16
choose the correct tool for measuring an object.	17
measure the same object using different units.	18
estimate the length of an object.	19
compare lengths to tell which object is longer and how much longer it is.	20
add and subtract lengths to solve problems.	21
measure lengths and show data on a line plot.	22
draw and solve problems with picture graphs and bar graphs.	23
tell and write time to the nearest 5 minutes.	24
solve problems about money.	25

Use these skills to solve Problems 1–6.

1 Sophie ate at the time shown on the clock. Show this time on the digital clock. Be sure to show whether it is AM or PM.

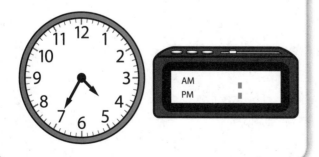

2 Which is the best estimate for the length of a baseball bat?

A 9 feet

B 12 centimeters

C 30 inches

D 50 meters

Solve.

3 Which number sentence could you use to find the difference in the lengths of the pieces of yarn? Circle all the correct answers.

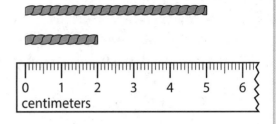

A 2 + ? = 5   **C** 7 − 5 = ?

B 5 + ? = 7   **D** 5 − 2 = ?

4 Ann asked some of her friends, "What is your favorite animal?" Then she made this bar graph.

How many fewer friends chose birds than cats?

A 1   **C** 3

B 2   **D** 4

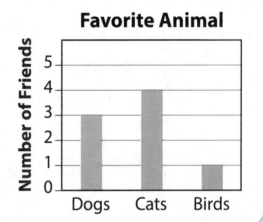

Favorite Animal

5 Ann asked 2 more friends to tell her their favorite animal. They both chose dogs. Fill in the graph in Problem 4 to show that 2 more friends chose dogs.

6 An eraser costs 27¢. Jim buys two erasers and uses three quarters to pay for them. Which coins could he get back in change? Circle all the correct answers.

A

C

B

D

Name: _____

Answer the questions and show all your work on separate paper.

Mindy makes mittens. She needs data about children's hand sizes. So, she asks your class for help.

Here is what Mindy wants you to do:

- Put your hand on a piece of paper. Mark the paper at the tip of your longest finger. Make another mark at your wrist.

- Make marks at each side of your hand by the knuckles.

- Use the marks to measure the length of your hand in centimeters. Then measure the width. Record the measurements.

- Collect length and width measurements from 7 classmates.

Use the tools on the back of this page.

- Make two line plots to organize the data.

- Use the sentence starters to help you write a report to Mindy. Give the shortest length and width and the longest length and width. Tell her which lengths and widths you found most often.

Reflect on Mathematical Practices

Use Tools to Measure Why did it help to mark the lengths on paper before measuring?

Checklist

Did you . . .

☐ record and label your measurements?

☐ check that your line plot matches the data?

☐ describe the data?

Word Bank Here are some words that you can use in your answer.

measure	length	width
line plot	centimeters	about
longest	shortest	widest

Models Here are some tools and models that you can use to find the solution.

Hand Lengths

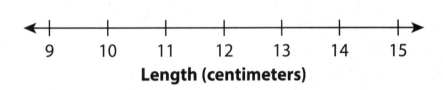

9   10   11   12   13   14   15

Length (centimeters)

Name	Hand Length	Hand Width

Sentence Starters Here are some sentence starters that might help you write your report.

The longest _____

The shortest _____

The length I found most often _____

Unit 3 Vocabulary

Name: _____

My Examples

inch

a unit of length. A quarter is about 1 inch across.

centimeter

a unit of lenth. Your little finger is about 1 centimeter across.

to estimate

math thinking to make a close guess

estimate

close guess made using math thinking

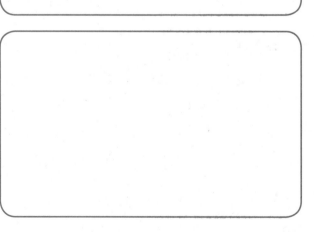

picture graph

a way to show data using pictures

bar graph

a way to show data using bars

data

a set of collected information

hour

a unit of time equal to 60 minutes

hour hand

the shorter hand on a clock. It shows hours.

minute hand

the longer hand on a clock. It shows minutes.

My Words

_____

_____

_____

_____

_____

_____

My Words

My Examples

Dear Family,

This week your child is learning about recognizing and drawing shapes by paying attention to the number of sides and angles they have.

Triangles have 3 sides and 3 angles.

Quadrilaterals have 4 sides and 4 angles.

rectangle   square   rhombus   trapezoid

Pentagons have 5 sides and 5 angles.

Hexagons have 6 sides and 6 angles.

Shapes can also be combined to create other shapes. See below for some examples of triangles, rectangles, rhombuses, and trapezoids combined to form a hexagon.

Invite your child to share what he or she knows about shapes by doing the following activity together.

NEXT

Materials: paper, crayons, or markers

Help your child become familiar with the names and attributes of various shapes by doing this activity together.

- Work with your child to draw the "wackiest" six-sided shape he or she can come up with.

- Help your child to split the shape into smaller shapes (use only triangles (3 sides), quadrilaterals (4 sides), and pentagons (5 sides)).

- Have your child color the shape using the following colors, or come up with a unique coloring pattern together.
  - Triangles = Red
  - Quadrilaterals = Blue
  - Pentagons = Yellow

- Ask your child how he or she identified each shape in order to color it in.

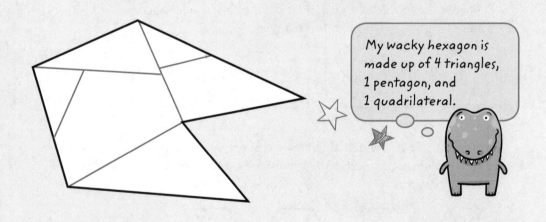

My wacky hexagon is made up of 4 triangles, 1 pentagon, and 1 quadrilateral.

Recognize and Draw Shapes

Name: _____

Study the example showing how to name a shape. Then solve Problems 1–3.

Example

A **triangle** has 3 sides and 3 corners.

A **rectangle** has 4 sides and 4 square corners.

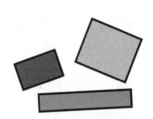

A **hexagon** has 6 sides and 6 corners.

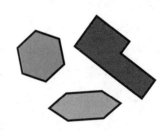

Write the number of sides and corners. Then write the name of the shape.

__3__ sides
__3__ corners

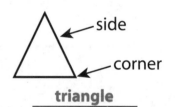

side

corner

_____triangle_____

---

1 Write the number of sides and corners.
Then write the name of the shape.

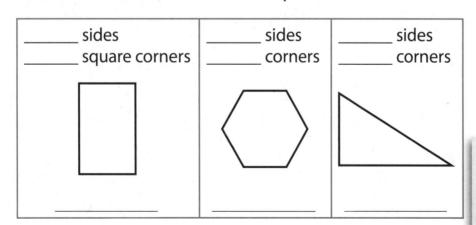

_____ sides
_____ square corners

_____ sides
_____ corners

_____ sides
_____ corners

_____

_____

_____

Vocabulary

side a straight line that is part of a shape.

A **rectangle** has 4 sides and 4 square corners.	A **rhombus** has 4 sides the same length and 4 corners.	A **square** has 4 sides the same length and 4 square corners.

Solve.

2 Write T in the blank if true. Write F in the blank if false. Then write the name of the shape.

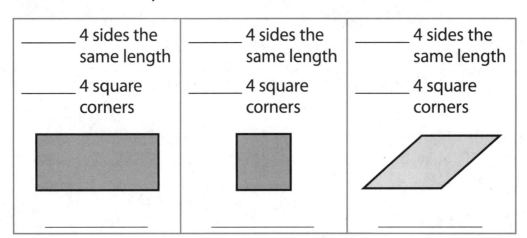

_____ 4 sides the same length	_____ 4 sides the same length	_____ 4 sides the same length
_____ 4 square corners	_____ 4 square corners	_____ 4 square corners

3 Bruce says this shape is a square. Do you agree? Why or why not?

_____

_____

_____

Name: _____

Name and Draw Shapes

Study the example showing how to name shapes and describe shapes. Then solve Problems 1–5.

Example

Quadrilaterals have 4 sides and 4 angles.

square

rectangle

trapezoid

rhombus

Pentagons have 5 sides and 5 angles.

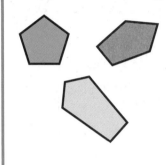

Hexagons have 6 sides and 6 angles.

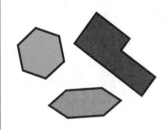

- What is the name of this shape?
- How many sides and angles does it have?

Shape name: rhombus
Number of sides: 4
Number of angles: 4

---

1 Look at the shapes below. Fill in the chart to name and describe each shape.

Shape A   Shape B   Shape C

Shape	Shape Name	Sides	Angles
A			
B			
C			

Vocabulary

angle the corner where two sides of a shape meet.

Solve.

2 Draw two different shapes that each have 3 sides. Then write the name for shapes with 3 sides.

Shape name: _____

3 Draw two different shapes that each have 6 angles. Then write the name for shapes with 6 angles.

Shape name: _____

4 Draw two different shapes that each have 5 sides. Then write the name for shapes with 5 sides.

Shape name: _____

5 Fill in the blanks. Use the words in the box.

| Some |
| No |
| All |

a. _____ quadrilaterals have 4 sides.

b. _____ quadrilaterals have 5 angles.

c. _____ quadrilaterals have sides the same length.

Name: _____

Make Shapes

Study the example showing how to use shapes to make other shapes. Then solve Problems 1–3.

Example

How can you use smaller shapes to make a trapezoid?

Look at the shapes in the green box.

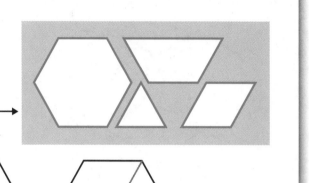

Draw lines to show the shapes you could use.

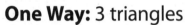

One Way: 3 triangles
Another Way: 1 rhombus and 1 triangle

---

1 The dotted lines show one way to make this shape from the smaller shapes. Draw lines to show another way. Then write the names of the shapes you use.

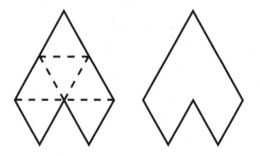

Shape names: _____

_____

Solve.

2 Draw lines to show how you could use shapes from the green box to make this shape. Then write the names of the shapes you use.

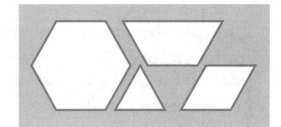

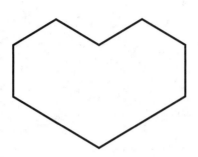

Shapes I used: _____

_____

3 Draw lines to show how you could use shapes from the green box to make this shape. Then write the names of the shapes you use.

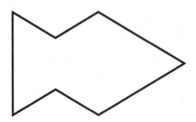

Shapes I used: _____

_____

Name: _____

Recognize and Draw Shapes

Solve the problems.

1 Circle *True* or *False* for each sentence.

You can draw a picture of each shape to help you.

a. All hexagons have
5 angles.   True   False

b. All squares have
4 equal sides.   True   False

c. All triangles have
3 equal sides.   True   False

d. All hexagons have
more sides than
triangles have.   True   False

2 Which shape has fewer sides than a
quadrilateral? Circle the correct answer.

How many sides does a quadrilateral have?

A pentagon   **C** triangle

B hexagon   **D** square

Nina chose **D**. This is wrong. Why is it
wrong?

_____

_____

_____

_____

Solve.

3 Draw a shape that has 6 sides. Write the name of the shape. You may use the dots to help you.

Show your work.

You can use the dots as the corners of your shape.

. . . .
. . . .
. . . .
. . . .
. . . .
. . . .

Answer: _____

4 What is the name of the big shape that is made by putting all of the small shapes together? How do you know?

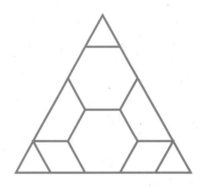

How many sides does the big shape have? How many angles does it have?

Answer: _____

5 There are 9 smaller shapes that make up the big shape in Problem 4. What are the smaller shapes? Write how many there are of each smaller shape.

You can draw a dot in each shape as you count it to keep track of the shapes you have counted.

_____ triangles   _____ pentagons

_____ quadrilaterals   _____ hexagons

Dear Family,

This week your child is exploring tiling rectangles with same-sized squares.

Rectangles can be tiled by squares in different ways. For example:

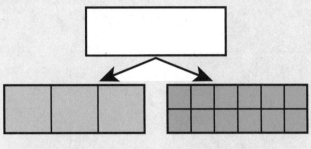

1 row and 3 columns	2 rows and 6 columns
3 large squares	12 small squares

Your child is exploring tiling rectangles to get ready for learning how to find the area of rectangles next year.

Examples of tiling can be found throughout your daily life. You may find square tiles covering the kitchen floor, the bathroom wall, or a ceiling. You may see squares filling a game board or a wall calendar.

Invite your child to share what he or she knows about tiling by doing the following activity together.

JUNE						
	1	2	3	4	5	6
7	8	9	10	11	12	13
14	15	16	17	18	19	20
21	22	23	24	25	26	27
28	29	30				

Materials: markers or crayons

• Work with your child to complete the two tilings shown below.

• Ask your child to count the number of rows and columns in each tiling.

• Ask your child which tiling is made up of more squares.

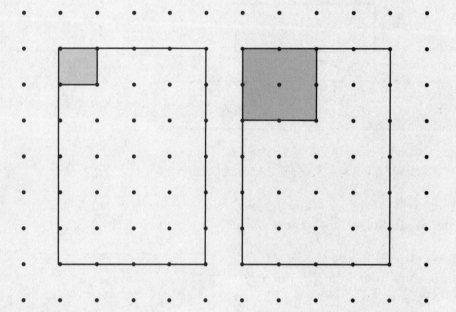

When I tile a rectangle with equal squares, the squares must fill up the whole rectangle and must not go outside the edges of the rectangle.

Name: _____

Prerequisite: **How can you put shapes together to make other shapes?**

Study the example showing how to put shapes together to make other shapes. Then solve Problems 1–4.

Example

How can you use smaller shapes to make a circle?

Look at the shapes in the green box.

Draw lines to show how you could use the shapes.

Write how many of each shape you would need.

_____2_____ ⌣   _____4_____ ◗

---

1 Draw a line to show how you could use squares like the one in the green box to make a rectangle. How many squares would you need?

_____ squares

---

2 Draw lines to show how you could use triangles like the one in the green box to make a rectangle. How many triangles would you need?

_____ triangles

Solve.

3 Draw lines to show how you could use hexagons to make the first shape below. Then show how you could use trapezoids to make the second shape. How many of each shape would you need?

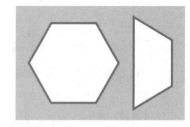

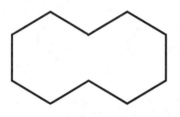   

_____ hexagons   _____ trapezoids

4 Draw lines to show how you could use triangles to make the first shape below. Then show how you could use trapezoids to make the second shape. Then show how you could use rhombuses to make the third shape. How many of each shape would you need?

_____ triangles   _____ trapezoids   _____ rhombuses

Name: _____

Draw and Count Squares

Study the example showing how to draw and count squares. Then solve Problems 1–8.

Example

Sal drew squares on dot paper to fill a rectangle. How many squares did he draw in all?

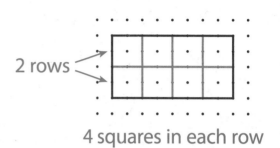

2 rows

4 squares in each row

- You can count each square.
- Or you can count the rows and number of squares in each row. Then add: 4 + 4 = ?

Sal drew 8 squares in all.

Answer the questions below to find how many squares are in the rectangle.

1 How many rows of squares are there?

_____ rows

2 How many squares are in each row?

_____ squares

3 What number sentence can you write to find how many squares in all?

_____ + _____ + _____ + _____ + _____ + _____ + _____ = _____

4 How many squares are in the rectangle?

_____ squares

Solve.

5 Write a number sentence to find how many squares are in the rectangle.

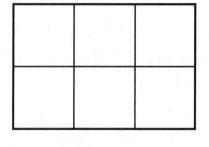

_____ + _____ + _____ = _____

How many squares are in the rectangle?

_____ squares

6 Write a number sentence to find how many squares are in the rectangle.

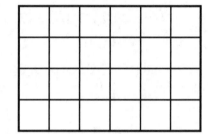

_____

How many squares are in the rectangle?

_____ squares

7 The rectangles in Problems 5 and 6 are the same size. Why does the rectangle in Problem 6 have more squares?

_____

_____

_____

8 Draw lines to show two different ways to fill the rectangles with same-sized squares.

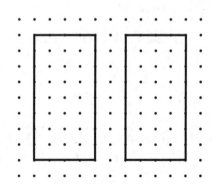

Name: _____

Reason and Write

Look at the example. Underline a part that you think makes it a good answer.

Example

Gwen drew this rectangle.

Gwen wrote, There are a total of 10 squares in my rectangle.

What did Gwen do right? What did she do wrong? Use pictures, words, or numbers to explain.

Gwen drew a rectangle correctly. Rectangles have 4 sides and 4 square corners. Gwen also filled her rectangle correctly because all of the shapes inside the rectangle are squares. Squares have 4 equal sides and 4 square corners like this.

Gwen's only mistake was writing that there are a total of 10 squares. Gwen should have counted to find that there are 2 rows of squares and 6 squares in each row. Then she could have added 6 + 6. Or she should have just counted all the squares to find that there are a total of 12 squares.

Where does the example . . .

- *answer both parts of the question?*
- *use words to explain?*
- *use numbers to explain?*
- *use a picture to explain?*

Solve the problem. Use what you learned from the example.

Nick drew this rectangle.

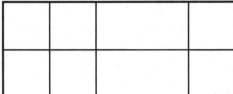

Nick wrote, There are a total of 8 squares in my rectangle.

What did Nick do right? What did he do wrong?

Show your work. Use pictures, words, or numbers to explain.

Did you . . .

• answer both parts of the question?

• use words to explain?

• use numbers to explain?

• use a picture to explain?

Dear Family,

This week your child is exploring the idea of equal parts of whole rectangles and circles to get ready for working with fractions next year.

Your child will see whole rectangles and circles cut into 2, 3, or 4 equal parts.

2 equal parts are called **halves**. Each of these parts is called one half of the whole.

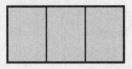

3 equal parts are called **thirds**. Each of these parts is called one third of the whole.

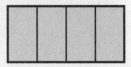

4 equal parts are called **fourths**. Each of these parts is called one fourth of the whole.

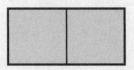

Invite your child to to share what he or she knows about halves, thirds, and fourths by doing the following activity together.

Along with your child, make a sandwich using square pieces of bread.

- Ask your child to show with his or her finger how to cut the sandwich into halves. Ask your child to show you more than one way. Talk about how many pieces there would be if you cut the sandwich into halves.

- Ask your child to show you how to cut the sandwich into thirds and fourths. Talk about how many pieces there would be if you cut the sandwich into thirds or into fourths.

- Ask your child how he or she would like the sandwich divided and cut the sandwich accordingly.

I like my sandwich cut in fourths. Here are three different ways I could cut my sandwich.

Name: _____

Prerequisite: How can you break shapes into equal parts?

Study the example showing how to draw equal parts. Then solve Problems 1–8.

Draw 4 equal parts. Circle the word that describes the parts.

halves

(fourths)

half of the whole

2 equal parts

fourth of the whole

4 equal parts

1 Draw 2 equal parts. Circle the word that describes the parts.

halves

fourths

2 Write how many equal parts. Circle the word that describes the parts.

halves

fourths

_____ equal parts

3 Write how many equal parts. Circle the word that describes the parts.

halves

fourths

_____ equal parts

Solve.

4 Draw 2 equal parts. Circle the word that describes the parts.

halves

fourths

5 Draw 4 equal parts. Circle the word that describes the parts.

halves

fourths

6 Draw 2 equal parts a different way than you did in Problem 4.

7 Draw 4 equal parts a different way than you did in Problem 5.

8 Vicky says she shaded half of this square. Do you agree? Why or why not?

_____

_____

_____

_____

_____

Name: _____

Divide Rectangles into Halves, Thirds, and Fourths

Study the example showing how to divide a rectangle into equal parts. Then solve Problems 1–9.

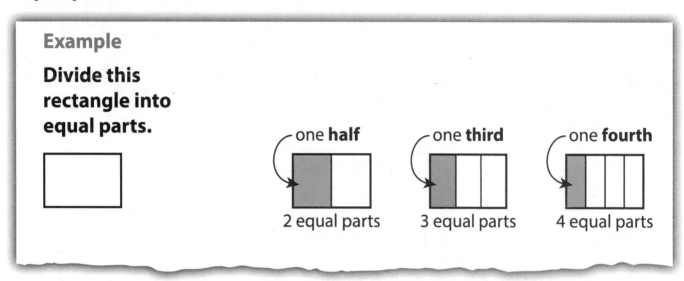

Example

Divide this rectangle into equal parts.

one **half**
2 equal parts

one **third**
3 equal parts

one **fourth**
4 equal parts

---

1 Divide this rectangle into two equal parts.

2 Circle the word to the right that makes this sentence true about the rectangle in Problem 1.

Each part is a _____ of the whole rectangle.

half

third

fourth

3 Show another way to divide a rectangle into two equal parts.

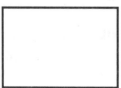

Lesson 28 Understand Halves, Thirds, and Fourths in Shapes

Solve.

4 Divide this rectangle into three equal parts.

5 Circle the word to the right that makes this sentence true about the rectangle in Problem 4.

Each part is a _____ of the whole rectangle.

half

third

fourth

6 Show another way to divide a rectangle into three equal parts.

7 Divide this rectangle into four equal parts.

8 Circle the word to the right that makes this sentence true about the rectangle in Problem 7.

Each part is a _____ of the whole rectangle.

half

third

fourth

9 Show another way to divide a rectangle into four equal parts.

Reason and Write

Look at the example. Underline a part that you think makes it a good answer.

Example

Cho drew these circles.

Cho wrote, My picture shows that a pie cut in thirds has bigger pieces than the same pie cut in half.

What did Cho do right? What did he do wrong? Use pictures, words, or numbers to explain.

Cho showed thirds and halves correctly. The first circle is divided into 3 equal parts. The second circle is divided into 2 equal parts.

Cho's mistake was that he drew the circles different sizes. He should have drawn the circles the same size. That is because he is trying to show the same pie cut two different ways.

Cho should have drawn his circles like this. Then he would see that a pie cut in thirds has smaller pieces than the same pie cut in half.

Where does the example . . .

- *answer both parts of the question?*
- *use words to explain?*
- *use numbers to explain?*
- *use a picture to explain?*

Solve the problem. Use what you learned from the example.

Alma drew these squares.

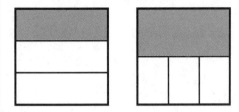

Alma wrote, My picture shows that a cracker broken into thirds has smaller pieces than the same cracker broken into fourths.

What did Alma do right? What did she do wrong?

Show your work. Use pictures, words, or numbers to explain.

Did you . . .

• answer both parts of the question?

• use words to explain?

• use numbers to explain?

• use a picture to explain?

Unit 4 Game

Shape Match

What you need: Recording Sheet, Word Cards and Shape Cards

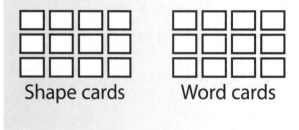

Directions

- Mix the Shape Cards. Lay them face down in 3 rows of 4 cards.

- Then mix the Word Cards. Lay them face down in 3 rows of 4 cards. Keep a space between the two groups of cards.

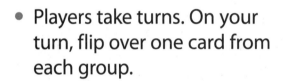

Shape cards   Word cards

- Players take turns. On your turn, flip over one card from each group.

- If the cards match, keep them. On the Recording Sheet, write what your Word Card says. Then draw a new shape that matches your Word Card.

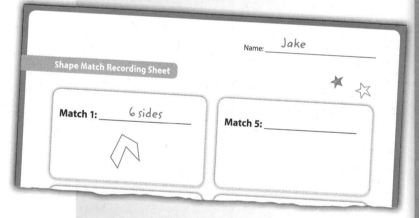

Name: Jake

Shape Match Recording Sheet

Match 1: ___6 sides___

Match 5: _____

- If the cards do not match, put them back, face down.

- Play until the cards are gone. The player with the most cards wins.

I got a match! I wrote "6 sides," then I drew a new shape with 6 sides.

Shape Match Recording Sheet

Match 1: _____

Match 5: _____

Match 2: _____

Match 6: _____

Match 3: _____

Match 7: _____

Match 4: _____

Match 8: _____

triangle	quadrilateral	pentagon	hexagon
3 sides	4 sides	5 sides	6 sides
3 angles	4 angles	5 angles	6 angles

Geometry

In this unit you learned to:	Lesson
recognize and draw different shapes.	26
break up a rectangle into squares.	27
divide shapes into equal parts.	28

Use these skills to solve Problems 1–7.

1 Trina drew a rectangle on a piece of paper. Circle *True* or *False* for each statement below about the shape Trina drew.

  a. It must have 4 equal sides.   True   False

  b. It is a quadrilateral.   True   False

  c. It can be made from 2 triangles.   True   False

  d. It has more angles than a pentagon.   True   False

2 Stan drew these lines on a grid to fill a rectangle with same-size squares. Draw lines on the other grid to show a different way to fill the rectangle with same-sized squares.

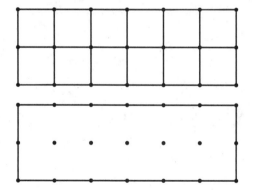

3 How many squares did Stan make in Problem 2? _____

4 How many squares did you make in Problem 2? _____

Solve.

5 What is true about the shape at the right? Circle all the correct answers.

  A It is a quadrilateral.

  B It can be made up of 1 hexagon and 1 triangle.

  C It can be made up of 2 trapezoids and 1 triangle.

  D It can be made up of 7 triangles.

6 Four friends want to share a sandwich. How can they divide the sandwich so that they all get the same amount? Circle all the correct answers.

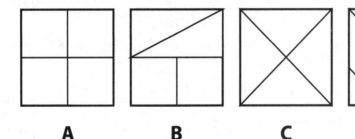

    A   **B**   **C**   **D**

7 Bri says she divided this circle into thirds. Do you agree or disagree? Explain.

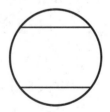

_____

_____

_____

_____

Name: _____

Answer the questions and show all your work on separate paper.

Tani has square sheets of colored paper. She is going to cut the paper and use the pieces to make an art project. This is what she wants to do:

- Divide each square into 2, 3, or 4 equal parts.

- Make parts that are different shapes.

- Make 12 parts altogether.

Show how she can cut the sheets of paper. Describe the shapes that you make. How many sheets of paper does your plan need?

Use the tools on the back of this page.

- Draw squares. Choose either 2, 3, or 4 equal parts. Then divide the squares into that number of equal parts. Divide the squares into different shapes.

- Use the sentence starters to help you describe the shapes you made.

- Tell how many sheets of paper your plan needs.

Reflect on Mathematical Practices

Look for Structure Three same-size squares are divided into 2, 3, and 4 equal parts. How does the number of parts relate to sizes of the parts?

Checklist

Did you . . .

☐ use the same number of equal parts in each square?

☐ describe the shapes?

☐ tell the number of sheets of paper you need?

Performance Task Tips

Word Bank Here are some words that you might use in your answer.

square	rectangle	triangle
half	third	fourth

Models Here are some models that you might use to find a solution.

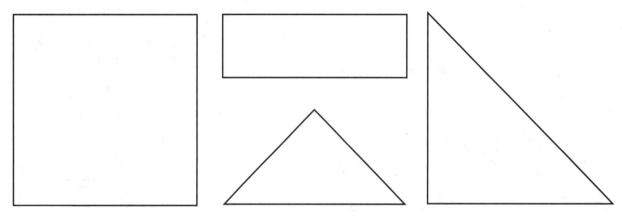

Sentence Starters Here are some sentence starters that can help describe your work.

I divided the squares _____

The parts _____

I used _____ sheets _____

Unit 4 Vocabulary

Name: _____

My Examples

side

a straight line that is part of a shape

angle

the corner where two sides of a shape meet

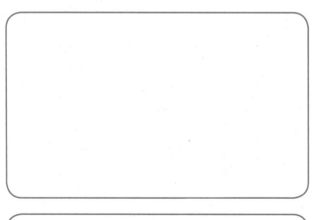

My Words

_____

_____

_____

_____

_____

_____

_____

My Words

My Examples

Fluency Table of Contents

Addition Facts—Skills Practice

Find sums to 10.   **Form A**

1 2 + 2 = _____   **2** 3 + 4 = _____   **3** 1 + 5 = _____

4 3 + 5 = _____   **5** 7 + 1 = _____   **6** 8 + 1 = _____

7 8 + 2 = _____   **8** 6 + 2 = _____   **9** 3 + 7 = _____

10 8 + 0 = _____   **11** 4 + 5 = _____   **12** 3 + 3 = _____

13 2 + 5 = _____   **14** 5 + 2 = _____   **15** 6 + 3 = _____

16 4 + 4 = _____   **17** 7 + 3 = _____   **18** 5 + 4 = _____

19 5 + 3 = _____   **20** 0 + 5 = _____   **21** 2 + 8 = _____

22 2 + 7 = _____   **23** 4 + 6 = _____   **24** 3 + 2 = _____

25 5 + 5 = _____   **26** 3 + 6 = _____   **27** 1 + 9 = _____

28 4 + 3 = _____   **29** 7 + 2 = _____   **30** 2 + 4 = _____

Addition Facts—Skills Practice

Find sums to 10.   **Form B**

1 $3 + 1 =$ _____   **2** $4 + 2 =$ _____   **3** $7 + 2 =$ _____

4 $5 + 5 =$ _____   **5** $3 + 2 =$ _____   **6** $9 + 1 =$ _____

7 $6 + 3 =$ _____   **8** $6 + 4 =$ _____   **9** $0 + 7 =$ _____

10 $4 + 4 =$ _____ **11** $5 + 3 =$ _____ **12** $1 + 5 =$ _____

13 $4 + 6 =$ _____ **14** $2 + 8 =$ _____ **15** $3 + 3 =$ _____

16 $9 + 0 =$ _____ **17** $3 + 5 =$ _____ **18** $2 + 6 =$ _____

19 $3 + 4 =$ _____ **20** $7 + 3 =$ _____ **21** $2 + 5 =$ _____

22 $6 + 1 =$ _____ **23** $8 + 2 =$ _____ **24** $3 + 6 =$ _____

25 $1 + 4 =$ _____ **26** $4 + 5 =$ _____ **27** $3 + 7 =$ _____

28 $6 + 2 =$ _____ **29** $1 + 6 =$ _____ **30** $5 + 4 =$ _____

Addition Facts—Skills Practice

Find sums from 11 to 20.   **Form A**

1 6 + 6 = _____   **2** 6 + 7 = _____   **3** 9 + 2 = _____

4 8 + 3 = _____   **5** 4 + 8 = _____   **6** 8 + 8 = _____

7 9 + 6 = _____   **8** 7 + 6 = _____   **9** 8 + 5 = _____

10 9 + 3 = _____   **11** 4 + 9 = _____   **12** 9 + 9 = _____

13 5 + 9 = _____   **14** 7 + 4 = _____   **15** 7 + 8 = _____

16 8 + 4 = _____   **17** 5 + 6 = _____   **18** 4 + 7 = _____

19 9 + 8 = _____   **20** 9 + 4 = _____   **21** 8 + 6 = _____

22 6 + 5 = _____   **23** 7 + 9 = _____   **24** 7 + 5 = _____

25 6 + 8 = _____   **26** 7 + 7 = _____   **27** 8 + 9 = _____

28 8 + 7 = _____   **29** 9 + 5 = _____   **30** 5 + 7 = _____

Addition Facts—Skills Practice

Find sums from 11 to 20.

Form B

1 $9 + 2 =$ _____

2 $9 + 6 =$ _____

3 $6 + 5 =$ _____

4 $5 + 8 =$ _____

5 $8 + 8 =$ _____

6 $9 + 3 =$ _____

7 $7 + 6 =$ _____

8 $3 + 8 =$ _____

9 $5 + 9 =$ _____

10 $8 + 4 =$ _____

11 $6 + 6 =$ _____

12 $9 + 7 =$ _____

13 $3 + 9 =$ _____

14 $7 + 7 =$ _____

15 $5 + 6 =$ _____

16 $9 + 8 =$ _____

17 $4 + 9 =$ _____

18 $8 + 6 =$ _____

19 $9 + 5 =$ _____

20 $6 + 8 =$ _____

21 $9 + 9 =$ _____

22 $5 + 7 =$ _____

23 $7 + 9 =$ _____

24 $7 + 4 =$ _____

25 $8 + 3 =$ _____

26 $7 + 5 =$ _____

27 $7 + 8 =$ _____

28 $6 + 9 =$ _____

29 $9 + 4 =$ _____

30 $8 + 9 =$ _____

Addition Facts—Skills Practice

Find sums to 20.

1 $9 + 1 =$ _____

2 $8 + 4 =$ _____

3 $5 + 6 =$ _____

4 $2 + 7 =$ _____

5 $8 + 0 =$ _____

6 $6 + 8 =$ _____

7 $7 + 9 =$ _____

8 $5 + 5 =$ _____

9 $4 + 9 =$ _____

10 $6 + 4 =$ _____

11 $1 + 5 =$ _____

12 $3 + 3 =$ _____

13 $9 + 6 =$ _____

14 $5 + 4 =$ _____

15 $7 + 3 =$ _____

16 $0 + 2 =$ _____

17 $2 + 8 =$ _____

18 $9 + 8 =$ _____

19 $3 + 9 =$ _____

20 $7 + 8 =$ _____

21 $4 + 5 =$ _____

22 $2 + 2 =$ _____

23 $6 + 6 =$ _____

24 $2 + 9 =$ _____

25 $8 + 7 =$ _____

26 $1 + 8 =$ _____

27 $4 + 6 =$ _____

28 $3 + 4 =$ _____

29 $5 + 8 =$ _____

30 $9 + 9 =$ _____

Addition Facts—Skills Practice

Find sums to 20.

1 $4 + 2 =$ _____

2 $5 + 3 =$ _____

3 $8 + 5 =$ _____

4 $7 + 7 =$ _____

5 $9 + 4 =$ _____

6 $0 + 4 =$ _____

7 $8 + 2 =$ _____

8 $8 + 9 =$ _____

9 $2 + 5 =$ _____

10 $9 + 5 =$ _____

11 $3 + 7 =$ _____

12 $1 + 9 =$ _____

13 $8 + 8 =$ _____

14 $5 + 7 =$ _____

15 $4 + 4 =$ _____

16 $3 + 6 =$ _____

17 $9 + 2 =$ _____

18 $6 + 9 =$ _____

19 $1 + 9 =$ _____

20 $7 + 6 =$ _____

21 $4 + 8 =$ _____

22 $5 + 0 =$ _____

23 $2 + 3 =$ _____

24 $9 + 7 =$ _____

25 $7 + 4 =$ _____

26 $6 + 7 =$ _____

27 $4 + 3 =$ _____

28 $2 + 6 =$ _____

29 $5 + 9 =$ _____

30 $3 + 8 =$ _____

Addition Facts—Repeated Reasoning

Find patterns with sums near 10.

1 $5 + 5 =$ _____

2 $5 + 4 =$ _____

3 $4 + 5 =$ _____

4 $6 + 4 =$ _____

5 $6 + 3 =$ _____

6 _____ $+ 4 = 9$

7 $7 + 3 =$ _____

8 $7 +$ _____ $= 9$

9 $6 + 3 =$ _____

10 $8 + 2 =$ _____

11 $8 + 1 =$ _____

12 $7 + 2 =$ _____

13 $9 + 1 =$ _____

14 $9 + 0 =$ _____

15 _____ $+ 1 = 9$

16 $5 + 5 =$ _____

17 $5 + 6 =$ _____

18 $6 + 5 =$ _____

19 $4 + 6 =$ _____

20 $4 +$ _____ $= 11$

21 $5 + 6 =$ _____

22 $3 + 7 =$ _____

23 $3 + 8 =$ _____

24 $4 + 7 =$ _____

25 $2 + 8 =$ _____

26 $2 + 9 =$ _____

27 _____ $+ 8 = 11$

28 $1 + 9 =$ _____

29 $1 +$ _____ $= 11$

30 $2 + 9 =$ _____

How does knowing that $5 + 5 = 10$ help you find $5 + 4$? How does it help you find $5 + 6$?

_____

_____

_____

_____

Find patterns in adding 9.

1 10 + 4 = _____

2 9 + 4 = _____

3 10 + 7 = _____

4 9 + 7 = _____

5 10 + 2 = _____

6 9 + 2 = _____

7 10 + 6 = _____

8 9 + 6 = _____

9 10 + 3 = _____

10 9 + 3 = _____

11 10 + 8 = _____

12 9 + 8 = _____

13 10 + 5 = _____

14 9 + 5 = _____

15 10 + 9 = _____

16 9 + 9 = _____

17 4 + 10 = _____

18 4 + 9 = _____

19 7 + 10 = _____

20 7 + 9 = _____

21 2 + 10 = _____

22 2 + 9 = _____

23 6 + 10 = _____

24 6 + 9 = _____

25 3 + 10 = _____

26 3 + 9 = _____

27 5 + 10 = _____

28 5 + 9 = _____

29 8 + 10 = _____

30 8 + 9 = _____

How does knowing that 5 + 10 = 15 help you find 5 + 9? How does knowing that 8 + 10 = 18 help you find 8 + 9?

_____

_____

_____

_____

Subtraction Facts—Skills Practice

Subtract within 10.

Form A

1 $3 - 1 =$ _____

2 $5 - 4 =$ _____

3 $9 - 5 =$ _____

4 $6 - 3 =$ _____

5 $10 - 4 =$ _____

6 $4 - 2 =$ _____

7 $7 - 0 =$ _____

8 $9 - 8 =$ _____

9 $8 - 3 =$ _____

10 $8 - 6 =$ _____

11 $10 - 5 =$ _____

12 $9 - 1 =$ _____

13 $7 - 2 =$ _____

14 $4 - 1 =$ _____

15 $7 - 5 =$ _____

16 $9 - 9 =$ _____

17 $6 - 5 =$ _____

18 $10 - 7 =$ _____

19 $9 - 4 =$ _____

20 $8 - 7 =$ _____

21 $5 - 3 =$ _____

22 $2 - 2 =$ _____

23 $7 - 4 =$ _____

24 $10 - 1 =$ _____

25 $4 - 3 =$ _____

26 $9 - 6 =$ _____

27 $10 - 9 =$ _____

28 $8 - 2 =$ _____

29 $6 - 4 =$ _____

30 $9 - 3 =$ _____

Subtraction Facts—Skills Practice

Subtract within 10. **Form B**

1 $6 - 2 =$ _____ **2** $10 - 2 =$ _____ **3** $7 - 3 =$ _____

4 $7 - 6 =$ _____ **5** $8 - 4 =$ _____ **6** $4 - 4 =$ _____

7 $5 - 1 =$ _____ **8** $9 - 7 =$ _____ **9** $7 - 4 =$ _____

10 $8 - 5 =$ _____ **11** $10 - 9 =$ _____ **12** $8 - 2 =$ _____

13 $10 - 3 =$ _____ **14** $2 - 1 =$ _____ **15** $7 - 5 =$ _____

16 $1 - 0 =$ _____ **17** $5 - 2 =$ _____ **18** $9 - 6 =$ _____

19 $9 - 2 =$ _____ **20** $8 - 7 =$ _____ **21** $10 - 4 =$ _____

22 $8 - 1 =$ _____ **23** $4 - 2 =$ _____ **24** $6 - 4 =$ _____

25 $10 - 6 =$ _____ **26** $9 - 3 =$ _____ **27** $10 - 8 =$ _____

28 $7 - 5 =$ _____ **29** $3 - 2 =$ _____ **30** $9 - 5 =$ _____

Subtraction Facts—Skills Practice

Subtract from teen numbers.

Form A

1 $11 - 2 = $ _____

2 $14 - 7 = $ _____

3 $10 - 5 = $ _____

4 $13 - 8 = $ _____

5 $12 - 4 = $ _____

6 $11 - 9 = $ _____

7 $15 - 6 = $ _____

8 $11 - 5 = $ _____

9 $15 - 8 = $ _____

10 $12 - 3 = $ _____

11 $14 - 8 = $ _____

12 $12 - 7 = $ _____

13 $13 - 9 = $ _____

14 $11 - 4 = $ _____

15 $13 - 5 = $ _____

16 $16 - 7 = $ _____

17 $12 - 6 = $ _____

18 $14 - 9 = $ _____

19 $13 - 6 = $ _____

20 $18 - 9 = $ _____

21 $12 - 8 = $ _____

22 $15 - 9 = $ _____

23 $14 - 5 = $ _____

24 $17 - 9 = $ _____

25 $11 - 6 = $ _____

26 $12 - 9 = $ _____

27 $15 - 7 = $ _____

28 $14 - 9 = $ _____

29 $16 - 8 = $ _____

30 $12 - 5 = $ _____

Subtraction Facts—Skills Practice

Subtract from teen numbers.   **Form B**

1 $11 - 3 =$ _____   **2** $11 - 9 =$ _____   **3** $16 - 8 =$ _____

4 $14 - 9 =$ _____   **5** $12 - 7 =$ _____   **6** $13 - 4 =$ _____

7 $17 - 8 =$ _____   **8** $14 - 6 =$ _____   **9** $15 - 9 =$ _____

10 $12 - 5 =$ _____   **11** $13 - 7 =$ _____   **12** $11 - 6 =$ _____

13 $14 - 8 =$ _____   **14** $17 - 9 =$ _____   **15** $13 - 5 =$ _____

16 $11 - 2 =$ _____   **17** $13 - 9 =$ _____   **18** $15 - 7 =$ _____

19 $13 - 6 =$ _____   **20** $18 - 9 =$ _____   **21** $11 - 8 =$ _____

22 $16 - 9 =$ _____   **23** $12 - 6 =$ _____   **24** $15 - 6 =$ _____

25 $11 - 5 =$ _____   **26** $16 - 7 =$ _____   **27** $12 - 9 =$ _____

28 $14 - 7 =$ _____   **29** $10 - 5 =$ _____   **30** $11 - 7 =$ _____

Subtraction Facts—Skills Practice

Subtract within 20.

Form A

1 $9 - 3 = $ _____

2 $12 - 5 = $ _____

3 $10 - 4 = $ _____

4 $14 - 9 = $ _____

5 $16 - 8 = $ _____

6 $11 - 9 = $ _____

7 $13 - 7 = $ _____

8 $12 - 3 = $ _____

9 $6 - 2 = $ _____

10 $8 - 4 = $ _____

11 $5 - 1 = $ _____

12 $10 - 5 = $ _____

13 $17 - 9 = $ _____

14 $10 - 8 = $ _____

15 $15 - 6 = $ _____

16 $9 - 6 = $ _____

17 $11 - 2 = $ _____

18 $14 - 8 = $ _____

19 $12 - 4 = $ _____

20 $10 - 7 = $ _____

21 $9 - 0 = $ _____

22 $13 - 9 = $ _____

23 $8 - 3 = $ _____

24 $11 - 6 = $ _____

25 $7 - 4 = $ _____

26 $15 - 8 = $ _____

27 $5 - 4 = $ _____

28 $7 - 7 = $ _____

29 $18 - 9 = $ _____

30 $8 - 6 = $ _____

Subtraction Facts—Skills Practice

Subtract within 20.

1 $11 - 3 =$ _____

2 $4 - 2 =$ _____

3 $12 - 8 =$ _____

4 $5 - 3 =$ _____

5 $15 - 7 =$ _____

6 $13 - 5 =$ _____

7 $9 - 4 =$ _____

8 $10 - 1 =$ _____

9 $16 - 9 =$ _____

10 $11 - 8 =$ _____

11 $8 - 5 =$ _____

12 $14 - 6 =$ _____

13 $4 - 4 =$ _____

14 $4 - 0 =$ _____

15 $12 - 7 =$ _____

16 $10 - 3 =$ _____

17 $13 - 6 =$ _____

18 $11 - 5 =$ _____

19 $17 - 8 =$ _____

20 $10 - 9 =$ _____

21 $7 - 3 =$ _____

22 $12 - 6 =$ _____

23 $6 - 3 =$ _____

24 $14 - 5 =$ _____

25 $7 - 5 =$ _____

26 $15 - 9 =$ _____

27 $10 - 6 =$ _____

28 $14 - 7 =$ _____

29 $9 - 5 =$ _____

30 $13 - 8 =$ _____

Subtraction Facts—Repeated Reasoning

Find patterns when you subtract from 9 or 11.

1 $10 - 1 =$ _____   **2** $9 - 1 =$ _____   **3** $11 - 1 =$ _____

4 $10 - 2 =$ _____   **5** $9 - 2 =$ _____   **6** $11 - 2 =$ _____

7 $10 - 3 =$ _____   **8** $9 - 3 =$ _____   **9** $11 - 3 =$ _____

10 $10 - 4 =$ _____   **11** $9 - 4 =$ _____   **12** $11 - 4 =$ _____

13 $10 - 5 =$ _____   **14** $9 - 5 =$ _____   **15** $11 - 5 =$ _____

16 $10 - 6 =$ _____   **17** $9 - 6 =$ _____   **18** $11 - 6 =$ _____

19 $10 - 7 =$ _____   **20** $9 - 7 =$ _____   **21** $11 - 7 =$ _____

22 $10 - 8 =$ _____   **23** $9 - 8 =$ _____   **24** $11 - 8 =$ _____

25 $10 - 9 =$ _____   **26** $9 - 9 =$ _____   **27** $11 - 9 =$ _____

How does knowing that $10 - 8 = 2$ help you find $9 - 8$? How does it help you find $11 - 8$?

_____

_____

_____

_____

Subtraction Facts—Repeated Reasoning

Find patterns with differences of 9.

1 12 − 10 = _____

2 12 − 9 = _____

3 15 − 10 = _____

4 15 − 9 = _____

5 13 − 10 = _____

6 13 − _____ = 4

7 18 − 10 = _____

8 18 − 9 = _____

9 11 − 10 = _____

10 _____ − 9 = 2

11 17 − 10 = _____

12 17 − 9 = _____

13 14 − 10 = _____

14 14 − _____ = 5

15 12 − 2 = _____

16 11 − 2 = _____

17 13 − 3 = _____

18 _____ − 3 = 9

19 16 − 6 = _____

20 15 − 6 = _____

21 19 − 9 = _____

22 18 − _____ = 9

23 15 − 5 = _____

24 14 − 5 = _____

25 17 − 7 = _____

26 _____ − 7 = 9

27 14 − 4 = _____

28 13 − 4 = _____

29 18 − 8 = _____

30 17 − _____ = 9

How does knowing that 12 − 10 = 2 help you find 12 − 9? How does knowing that 15 − 10 = 5 help you find 15 − 9?

_____

_____

_____

_____

Name: _____

Add a 2-digit and a 1-digit number.

Form A

1	25 + 3	2	18 + 8	3	55 + 5	4	81 + 6
5	54 + 9	6	23 + 7	7	43 + 8	8	20 + 9
9	64 + 4	10	19 + 8	11	92 + 7	12	62 + 9
13	35 + 6	14	72 + 9	15	46 + 3	16	73 + 7
17	88 + 8	18	65 + 7	19	22 + 4	20	48 + 5

Addition Within 100—Skills Practice

Name: _____

Add a 2-digit and a 1-digit number.

Form B

1   12
     $+\ \ 5$

2   58
     $+\ \ 4$

3   29
     $+\ \ 6$

4   84
     $+\ \ 2$

5   67
     $+\ \ 3$

6   34
     $+\ \ 7$

7   91
     $+\ \ 8$

8   23
     $+\ \ 3$

9   75
     $+\ \ 8$

10   42
      $+\ \ 3$

11   59
      $+\ \ 9$

12   32
      $+\ \ 6$

13   29
      $+\ \ 3$

14   87
      $+\ \ 7$

15   44
      $+\ \ 6$

16   53
      $+\ \ 5$

17   18
      $+\ \ 9$

18   62
      $+\ \ 8$

19   79
      $+\ \ 7$

20   33
      $+\ \ 9$

Add 2-digit numbers.

Form A

1
```
  14
+ 14
```

2
```
  38
+ 17
```

3
```
  43
+ 39
```

4
```
  25
+ 32
```

5
```
  27
+ 23
```

6
```
  49
+ 46
```

7
```
  23
+ 65
```

8
```
  74
+ 18
```

9
```
  36
+ 34
```

10
```
  13
+ 18
```

11
```
  72
+ 27
```

12
```
  36
+ 28
```

13
```
  40
+ 19
```

14
```
  58
+ 23
```

15
```
  65
+ 16
```

16
```
  44
+ 33
```

17
```
  25
+ 31
```

18
```
  49
+ 49
```

19
```
  11
+ 18
```

20
```
  38
+ 45
```

Add 2-digit numbers.

Form B

1   22
    + 15

2   43
    + 19

3   36
    + 32

4   48
    + 48

5   17
    + 56

6   25
    + 55

7   33
    + 24

8   71
    + 19

9   63
    + 36

10   12
    + 34

11   20
    + 28

12   39
    + 17

13   25
    + 38

14   58
    + 29

15   45
    + 23

16   34
    + 56

17   69
    + 24

18   22
    + 66

19   73
    + 12

20   35
    + 37

Name: _____

Find regrouping patterns.

1 7 + 3 = _____   **2** 7 + 4 = _____   **3** 7 + 5 = _____

4 17 + 3 = _____   **5** 17 + 4 = _____   **6** 17 + 5 = _____

7 27 + 3 = _____   **8** 27 + 4 = _____   **9** 27 + 5 = _____

10 8 + 2 = _____   **11** 8 + 3 = _____   **12** 8 + 4 = _____

13 18 + 2 = _____   **14** 18 + 3 = _____   **15** 18 + 4 = _____

16 28 + 2 = _____   **17** 28 + 3 = _____   **18** 28 + 4 = _____

19 6 + 4 = _____   **20** 6 + 5 = _____   **21** 6 + 6 = _____

22 16 + 4 = _____   **23** 16 + 5 = _____   **24** 16 + 6 = _____

25 26 + 4 = _____   **26** 26 + 5 = _____   **27** 26 + 6 = _____

Look at Problems 1 to 9. How does knowing that 7 + 3 = 10 help you find 7 + 5? How does knowing that 7 + 3 = 10 help you find 27 + 5?

_____

_____

_____

_____

Addition Within 100—Repeated Reasoning

Name: _____

Find more regrouping patterns.

1 $30 + 1 + 40 + 9 =$ _____

2 $31 + 49 =$ _____

3 $30 + 2 + 40 + 8 =$ _____

4 $32 + 48 =$ _____

5 $30 + 3 + 40 + 7 =$ _____

6 $33 + 47 =$ _____

7 $20 + 4 + 30 + 6 =$ _____

8 $24 + 36 =$ _____

9 $20 + 5 + 30 + 5 =$ _____

10 $25 +$ _____ $= 60$

11 $20 + 6 + 30 + 4 =$ _____

12 _____ $+ 34 = 60$

13 $40 + 7 + 20 + 3 =$ _____

14 $47 + 23 =$ _____

15 $40 + 8 + 20 + 2 =$ _____

16 _____ $+ 22 = 70$

17 $40 + 9 + 20 + 1 =$ _____

18 $49 +$ _____ $= 70$

Look at Problems 7 and 8. How can knowing that $4 + 6 = 10$ help you find $24 + 36$?

_____

_____

_____

_____

Subtraction Within 100—Skills Practice

Subtract a 1-digit number from a 2-digit number.   **Form A**

1   49
      − 3
      ———

2   25
      − 7
      ———

3   56
      − 2
      ———

4   38
      − 9
      ———

5   88
      − 4
      ———

6   67
      − 6
      ———

7   41
      − 6
      ———

8   90
      − 8
      ———

9   73
      − 7
      ———

10   94
       − 3
       ———

11   86
       − 9
       ———

12   31
       − 1
       ———

13   52
       − 3
       ———

14   34
       − 5
       ———

15   27
       − 4
       ———

16   85
       − 3
       ———

17   99
       − 7
       ———

18   70
       − 4
       ———

19   48
       − 6
       ———

20   65
       − 8
       ———

Subtract a 1-digit number from a 2-digit number.

Form B

1
$$17$$
$$- 2$$

2
$$36$$
$$- 5$$

3
$$24$$
$$- 8$$

4
$$59$$
$$- 7$$

5
$$45$$
$$- 6$$

6
$$51$$
$$- 3$$

7
$$78$$
$$- 6$$

8
$$93$$
$$- 8$$

9
$$68$$
$$- 8$$

10
$$37$$
$$- 9$$

11
$$25$$
$$- 2$$

12
$$40$$
$$- 6$$

13
$$93$$
$$- 3$$

14
$$89$$
$$- 6$$

15
$$62$$
$$- 5$$

16
$$77$$
$$- 5$$

17
$$80$$
$$- 7$$

18
$$76$$
$$- 8$$

19
$$49$$
$$- 5$$

20
$$81$$
$$- 8$$

Name: _____

Subtract 2-digit numbers.

1
$$\begin{array}{r} 34 \\ -\ 12 \\ \hline \end{array}$$

2
$$\begin{array}{r} 75 \\ -\ 25 \\ \hline \end{array}$$

3
$$\begin{array}{r} 42 \\ -\ 18 \\ \hline \end{array}$$

4
$$\begin{array}{r} 67 \\ -\ 37 \\ \hline \end{array}$$

5
$$\begin{array}{r} 85 \\ -\ 26 \\ \hline \end{array}$$

6
$$\begin{array}{r} 51 \\ -\ 15 \\ \hline \end{array}$$

7
$$\begin{array}{r} 93 \\ -\ 72 \\ \hline \end{array}$$

8
$$\begin{array}{r} 96 \\ -\ 48 \\ \hline \end{array}$$

9
$$\begin{array}{r} 78 \\ -\ 20 \\ \hline \end{array}$$

10
$$\begin{array}{r} 63 \\ -\ 39 \\ \hline \end{array}$$

11
$$\begin{array}{r} 28 \\ -\ 14 \\ \hline \end{array}$$

12
$$\begin{array}{r} 34 \\ -\ 25 \\ \hline \end{array}$$

13
$$\begin{array}{r} 59 \\ -\ 48 \\ \hline \end{array}$$

14
$$\begin{array}{r} 86 \\ -\ 82 \\ \hline \end{array}$$

15
$$\begin{array}{r} 77 \\ -\ 28 \\ \hline \end{array}$$

16
$$\begin{array}{r} 33 \\ -\ 21 \\ \hline \end{array}$$

17
$$\begin{array}{r} 36 \\ -\ 19 \\ \hline \end{array}$$

18
$$\begin{array}{r} 95 \\ -\ 67 \\ \hline \end{array}$$

19
$$\begin{array}{r} 87 \\ -\ 44 \\ \hline \end{array}$$

20
$$\begin{array}{r} 58 \\ -\ 39 \\ \hline \end{array}$$

Subtraction Within 100—Skills Practice

Name: _____

Subtract 2-digit numbers.

Form B

1   37
   − 26

2   68
   − 41

3   53
   − 27

4   45
   − 15

5   76
   − 38

6   80
   − 47

7   94
   − 72

8   32
   − 17

9   99
   − 14

10   24
   − 15

11   87
   − 40

12   63
   − 28

13   53
   − 21

14   76
   − 33

15   95
   − 39

16   56
   − 42

17   86
   − 57

18   62
   − 24

19   48
   − 32

20   71
   − 43

Find place value patterns.

1 83 − 0 = _____   **2** 83 − 10 = _____   **3** 83 − 20 = _____

4 83 − 1 = _____   **5** 83 − 11 = _____   **6** 83 − 21 = _____

7 83 − 2 = _____   **8** 83 − 12 = _____   **9** 83 − 22 = _____

10 83 − 3 = _____   **11** 83 − 13 = _____   **12** 83 − 23 = _____

13 83 − 4 = _____   **14** 83 − 14 = _____   **15** 83 − 24 = _____

16 83 − 5 = _____   **17** 83 − 15 = _____   **18** 83 − 25 = _____

19 73 − 5 = _____   **20** 73 − 15 = _____   **21** 73 − 25 = _____

22 63 − 5 = _____   **23** 63 − 15 = _____   **24** 63 − 25 = _____

25 53 − 5 = _____   **26** 53 − 15 = _____   **27** 53 − 25 = _____

Look at Problems 25, 26, and 27. What is the same about the answers? What is different? How does knowing 53 − 25 help you find 53 − 35?

_____

_____

_____

©Curriculum Associates, LLC Copying is permitted for classroom use.

Name: _____

Find patterns with problems that have the same answer.

1 100 − 10 = _____

2 100 − 10 − 1 = _____

3 100 − 11 = _____

4 100 − 10 − 2 = _____

5 100 − 12 = _____

6 100 − 20 = _____

7 100 − 20 − 1 = _____

8 100 − 21 = _____

9 100 − 20 − 2 = _____

10 100 − 22 = _____

11 100 − 30 = _____

12 100 − 30 − 3 = _____

13 100 − 33 = _____

14 100 − 30 − 4 = _____

15 100 − 34 = _____

16 100 − 40 = _____

17 100 − 40 − 3 = _____

18 100 − 43 = _____

19 100 − 40 − 4 = _____

20 100 − 44 = _____

How does solving 100 − 40 − 3 help you find 100 − 43?

_____

_____

_____

_____

Name: _____

Add or subtract.

Form A

1 4 + 4 = _____

2 8 + 2 = _____

3 5 + 7 = _____

4 9 − 3 = _____

5 17 − 8 = _____

6 10 − 6 = _____

7
```
   21
 +  8
```

8
```
   37
 +  3
```

9
```
   84
 +  9
```

10
```
   72
 +  5
```

11
```
   45
 −  6
```

12
```
   58
 −  2
```

13
```
   98
 −  3
```

14
```
   61
 −  8
```

15
```
   12
 + 32
```

16
```
   39
 + 51
```

17
```
   26
 + 33
```

18
```
   57
 + 27
```

19
```
   83
 − 38
```

20
```
   74
 − 70
```

21
```
   52
 − 35
```

22
```
   49
 − 18
```

Add or subtract.

Form B

1 6 + 3 = _____

2 7 + 7 = _____

3 9 + 8 = _____

4 5 − 4 = _____

5 13 − 9 = _____

6 16 − 8 = _____

7
$$\begin{array}{r} 45 \\ + \ 6 \\ \hline \end{array}$$

8
$$\begin{array}{r} 23 \\ + \ 4 \\ \hline \end{array}$$

9
$$\begin{array}{r} 74 \\ + \ 5 \\ \hline \end{array}$$

10
$$\begin{array}{r} 59 \\ + \ 3 \\ \hline \end{array}$$

11
$$\begin{array}{r} 87 \\ - \ 3 \\ \hline \end{array}$$

12
$$\begin{array}{r} 62 \\ - \ 6 \\ \hline \end{array}$$

13
$$\begin{array}{r} 56 \\ - \ 5 \\ \hline \end{array}$$

14
$$\begin{array}{r} 94 \\ - \ 8 \\ \hline \end{array}$$

15
$$\begin{array}{r} 36 \\ + 60 \\ \hline \end{array}$$

16
$$\begin{array}{r} 29 \\ + 39 \\ \hline \end{array}$$

17
$$\begin{array}{r} 43 \\ + 32 \\ \hline \end{array}$$

18
$$\begin{array}{r} 67 \\ + 24 \\ \hline \end{array}$$

19
$$\begin{array}{r} 92 \\ - 53 \\ \hline \end{array}$$

20
$$\begin{array}{r} 78 \\ - 25 \\ \hline \end{array}$$

21
$$\begin{array}{r} 81 \\ - 64 \\ \hline \end{array}$$

22
$$\begin{array}{r} 97 \\ - 18 \\ \hline \end{array}$$

Addition and Subtraction Within 1,000— Skills Practice

Name: _____

Add and subtract 10 and 100.

Form A

1 24 + 10 = _____

2 375 + 100 = _____

3 580 + 10 = _____

4 77 − 10 = _____

5 238 − 100 = _____

6 462 − 10 = _____

7 44 + 10 = _____

8 727 + 100 = _____

9 703 + 10 = _____

10 86 − 10 = _____

11 446 − 100 = _____

12 112 − 10 = _____

13 59 + 10 = _____

14 500 + 100 = _____

15 633 + 10 = _____

16 73 − 10 = _____

17 874 − 100 = _____

18 808 − 10 = _____

19 15 + 10 = _____

20 702 + 100 = _____

21 451 + 10 = _____

22 90 − 10 = _____

23 357 − 100 = _____

24 234 − 10 = _____

25 61 + 10 = _____

26 555 + 100 = _____

27 290 + 10 = _____

28 32 − 10 = _____

29 692 − 100 = _____

30 989 − 10 = _____

Addition and Subtraction Within 1,000— Skills Practice

Name: _____

Add and subtract 10 and 100.

Form B

1 $37 + 10 =$ _____

2 $548 + 100 =$ _____

3 $472 + 10 =$ _____

4 $64 - 10 =$ _____

5 $841 - 100 =$ _____

6 $115 - 10 =$ _____

7 $85 + 10 =$ _____

8 $597 + 100 =$ _____

9 $712 + 10 =$ _____

10 $33 - 10 =$ _____

11 $608 - 100 =$ _____

12 $529 - 10 =$ _____

13 $70 + 10 =$ _____

14 $466 + 100 =$ _____

15 $903 + 10 =$ _____

16 $98 - 10 =$ _____

17 $230 - 100 =$ _____

18 $681 - 10 =$ _____

19 $56 + 10 =$ _____

20 $556 + 100 =$ _____

21 $199 + 10 =$ _____

22 $89 - 10 =$ _____

23 $303 - 100 =$ _____

24 $548 - 10 =$ _____

25 $41 + 10 =$ _____

26 $895 + 100 =$ _____

27 $890 + 10 =$ _____

28 $72 - 10 =$ _____

29 $771 - 100 =$ _____

30 $292 - 10 =$ _____

Addition and Subtraction Within 1,000—Skills Practice

Name: _____

Find sums up to 1,000.

Form A

1
$$213 + 462$$

2
$$129 + 625$$

3
$$465 + 173$$

4
$$257 + 584$$

5
$$379 + 381$$

6
$$163 + 507$$

7
$$228 + 334$$

8
$$148 + 775$$

9
$$543 + 321$$

10
$$427 + 273$$

11
$$284 + 284$$

12
$$530 + 292$$

13
$$354 + 119$$

14
$$172 + 682$$

15
$$393 + 105$$

16
$$297 + 569$$

17
$$237 + 557$$

18
$$421 + 124$$

19
$$389 + 538$$

20
$$654 + 156$$

Find sums up to 1,000.   **Form B**

1   614
    + 182

2   227
    + 325

3   191
    + 494

4   268
    + 357

5   123
    + 321

6   364
    + 279

7   242
    + 575

8   485
    + 241

9   587
    + 337

10   328
    + 612

11   649
    + 139

12   348
    + 384

13   428
    + 225

14   824
    + 142

15   375
    + 579

16   472
    + 336

17   152
    + 183

18   327
    + 237

19   341
    + 341

20   257
    + 696

Addition and Subtraction Within 1,000— Skills Practice

Name: _____

Subtract from 3-digit numbers.

Form A

1
$$843 - 721$$

2
$$556 - 229$$

3
$$659 - 484$$

4
$$932 - 346$$

5
$$480 - 326$$

6
$$851 - 548$$

7
$$941 - 184$$

8
$$868 - 787$$

9
$$982 - 561$$

10
$$600 - 312$$

11
$$835 - 232$$

12
$$765 - 275$$

13
$$517 - 158$$

14
$$835 - 232$$

15
$$363 - 289$$

16
$$935 - 617$$

17
$$748 - 272$$

18
$$616 - 414$$

19
$$528 - 174$$

20
$$957 - 379$$

Name: _____

Subtract from 3-digit numbers.

Form B

1 $\begin{array}{r} 595 \\ -383 \\ \hline \end{array}$	**2** $\begin{array}{r} 726 \\ -154 \\ \hline \end{array}$	**3** $\begin{array}{r} 644 \\ -119 \\ \hline \end{array}$	**4** $\begin{array}{r} 872 \\ -694 \\ \hline \end{array}$
5 $\begin{array}{r} 430 \\ -143 \\ \hline \end{array}$	**6** $\begin{array}{r} 956 \\ -927 \\ \hline \end{array}$	**7** $\begin{array}{r} 988 \\ -296 \\ \hline \end{array}$	**8** $\begin{array}{r} 349 \\ -187 \\ \hline \end{array}$
9 $\begin{array}{r} 873 \\ -367 \\ \hline \end{array}$	**10** $\begin{array}{r} 642 \\ -231 \\ \hline \end{array}$	**11** $\begin{array}{r} 516 \\ -238 \\ \hline \end{array}$	**12** $\begin{array}{r} 825 \\ -568 \\ \hline \end{array}$
13 $\begin{array}{r} 986 \\ -655 \\ \hline \end{array}$	**14** $\begin{array}{r} 822 \\ -288 \\ \hline \end{array}$	**15** $\begin{array}{r} 740 \\ -319 \\ \hline \end{array}$	**16** $\begin{array}{r} 434 \\ -373 \\ \hline \end{array}$
17 $\begin{array}{r} 605 \\ -183 \\ \hline \end{array}$	**18** $\begin{array}{r} 597 \\ -355 \\ \hline \end{array}$	**19** $\begin{array}{r} 962 \\ -437 \\ \hline \end{array}$	**20** $\begin{array}{r} 784 \\ -295 \\ \hline \end{array}$

Add several 2-digit numbers.

Form A

1)
```
   14
   37
+ 16
```

2)
```
   20
   73
+ 30
```

3)
```
   75
   96
+ 25
```

4)
```
   13
   22
+ 24
```

5)
```
   32
   65
+ 48
```

6)
```
   46
   77
+ 56
```

7)
```
   28
   63
+ 42
```

8)
```
   39
   61
+ 18
```

9)
```
   31
   24
   11
+ 23
```

10)
```
   42
   24
   58
+ 24
```

11)
```
   20
   32
   18
+ 40
```

12)
```
   66
   44
   33
+ 11
```

13)
```
   25
   12
   25
+ 13
```

14)
```
   23
   54
   37
+ 16
```

15)
```
   49
   28
   28
+ 49
```

16)
```
   32
   45
   17
+ 68
```

Add several 2-digit numbers.

Form B

1
```
  22
  10
+ 32
```

2
```
  25
  95
+ 25
```

3
```
  46
  83
+ 54
```

4
```
  35
  19
+ 21
```

5
```
  84
  34
+ 45
```

6
```
  71
  72
+ 15
```

7
```
  27
  56
+ 43
```

8
```
  67
  78
+ 22
```

9
```
  34
  12
  36
+ 13
```

10
```
  14
  13
  12
+ 11
```

11
```
  58
  27
  42
+ 27
```

12
```
  73
  35
  17
+ 45
```

13
```
  42
  24
  81
+ 18
```

14
```
  36
  25
  75
+ 63
```

15
```
  33
  20
  30
+ 44
```

16
```
  59
  42
  39
+ 21
```

Addition and Subtraction Within 1,000— Repeated Reasoning

Name: _____

Find place value patterns in addition.

1 4 + 4 = _____

2 40 + 40 = _____

3 400 + 400 = _____

4 2 + 5 = _____

5 20 + 50 = _____

6 200 + 500 = _____

7 6 + 3 = _____

8 60 + 30 = _____

9 600 + 300 = _____

10 100 + 50 = _____

11 100 + 50 + 100 + 50 = _____

12 150 + 150 = _____

13 400 + 20 = _____

14 400 + 20 + 400 + 20 = _____

15 420 + 420 = _____

16 300 + 40 = _____

17 300 + 40 + 300 + 40 = _____

18 340 + 340 = _____

How does finding 100 + 50 + 100 + 50 help you find 150 + 150?

_____

_____

_____

Find place value patterns in subtraction.

1 $3 - 2 =$ _____

2 $30 - 20 =$ _____

3 $300 - 200 =$ _____

4 $9 - 5 =$ _____

5 $90 - 50 =$ _____

6 $900 - 500 =$ _____

7 $6 - 4 =$ _____

8 $60 - 40 =$ _____

9 $600 - 400 =$ _____

10 $400 - 100 =$ _____

11 $400 - 100 - 50 =$ _____

12 $400 - 150 =$ _____

13 $800 - 600 =$ _____

14 $800 - 600 - 20 =$ _____

15 $800 - 620 =$ _____

16 $700 - 300 =$ _____

17 $700 - 300 - 60 =$ _____

18 $700 - 360 =$ _____

Look at Problems 7, 8, and 9. What is the same about each answer? What is different? How does knowing that $6 - 4 = 2$ help you find $60 - 40$ and $600 - 400$?

_____

_____

_____

_____

_____